PSYCHOLOGY FOR EVERYMAN

Larry Skurnik was born in New York City and educated in the U.S.A., obtaining his Ph.D. from Purdue University in 1962. He has been engaged in university teaching, T.V. script writing, market research and educational research with the National Foundation for Educational Research in England and Wales. He has more recently been employed by the American Institutes for Research as an adviser to the West African Examinations Council. Dr Skurnik is the author and co-author of a number of publications in the field of psychology and education.

Frank George was educated at Taunton School and Sidney Sussex College, Cambridge. He read the Moral Sciences Tripos and the Mathematics Tripos. He was Visitor at McGill University in 1953, Visiting Professor at Princeton University in 1953–4, and Visitor to the University of California at Los Angeles in 1962. He taught at Bristol University for nineteen years and during the last nine was a director of a number of scientific companies. In 1968 he was appointed Professor of Cybernetics and Director of the Institute of Cybernetics at Brunel University. He has a wide range of interests in all aspects of cybernetics, as well as logic and philosophy. He is married and has two daughters.

Psychology For Everyman

*

LARRY S. SKURNIK

FRANK GEORGE

PENGUIN BOOKS

Penguin Books Ltd, Harmondsworth, Middlesex, England
Penguin Books, 625 Madison Avenue, New York, New York 10022, U.S.A.
Penguin Books Australia Ltd, Ringwood, Victoria, Australia
Penguin Books Canada Ltd, 2801 John Street, Markham, Ontario, Canada L3R 1B4
Penguin Books (N.Z.) Ltd, 182–190 Wairau Road, Auckland 10, New Zealand

—

First published 1964
Second edition 1967
Reprinted 1969, 1970, 1972, 1974, 1975, 1977, 1979

—

—

Made and printed in Great Britain
by Hazell Watson & Viney Ltd,
Aylesbury, Bucks
Set in Linotype Granjon

CONTENTS

LIST OF PLATES

PREFACE TO THE SECOND EDITION

THIS book was originally prepared as a supporting text for a series of twenty-six television programmes, produced by A B C - T V, called Psychology for Everyman. Both the series and this book present to the layman some of the basic concepts in psychology. The ideas, facts, and evidence that have been accumulated by psychologists over the years have been simplified, and only a small portion have been presented. We have tried, as far as possible, to present concepts and ideas which are likely to be both interesting and helpful to the reader and viewer, but we have also included some of the more complicated theories in the field, so that more than a few bare bones of information are presented. It is hoped that this approach will lead to clearer insight into people's own behaviour, and greater understanding of the actions and motives of others.

The authors wish to express their gratitude to the producer of the T V series, Geoffrey Gilbert, for the generous wisdom and guidance that he provided. The series could not have succeeded without his ideas and insights and those of his team at A B C - T V, who are too numerous to mention. We also appreciate the careful reading and comments on the first edition in manuscript made by Mr Alan Snyder of the U.S. Air Force and also Mr Peter Powesland of the University of Bristol.

The immediate success of the first edition has encouraged us to develop the text and to add some illustrations. The addition of very short Further Reading lists to each chapter and the inclusion of an index will, we hope, consolidate the usefulness of the book as a first 'bird's-eye view' of the world of psychology.

Larry S. Skurnik
Frank George

1966

CHAPTER ONE

THE METHODS OF PSYCHOLOGY

THE word 'psychology' is made up from two Greek words: *psyche*, meaning mind or soul, and *logos* meaning word or study. 'Psychology', then, means 'the study of the mind', and this is one way of describing what psychologists try to do. There is, however, a serious difficulty with this definition. No one has been able to isolate or identify 'the mind' scientifically. It has no known weight or size and does not appear to exist in any material form. 'Mind' is a left-over term from an earlier century when it was thought that man was controlled by some small creature or spirit within. Later this idea was modified and mind was thought of as some operating and controlling process which was different from the body. The two were thought to work in harness together. This approach merely pursued an elusive abstraction, so psychologists, as scientists, shifted their attention to a more concrete approach to the study of man. They began to concentrate upon the observable *effects* of the 'mind' – that is, the way in which we behave.

Psychology may be defined, then, as the scientific study of the behaviour of man and other animals. It is not the only branch of science which examines people, but psychology differs from other disciplines in that it is concerned chiefly with *behaviour*. It is man's performance in which psychologists are primarily interested. But they also try to relate their theories of behaviour to what is known of the structure and workings of the body. This is not at all easy, since the human body is very complex. The brain, to look at just one of its working parts, has over 10,000,000,000 components (cells), and each of these may have a number of different connexions. At our present level of knowledge, it is impossible to specify how every individual cell functions. The most the scientist can do at the moment is to select some of the complex acts that are performed by humans and, with patience and study, identify some of the processes which seem to govern this behaviour.

This emphasis upon precise, measurable evidence, has produced useful results in understanding, predicting, and controlling human behaviour, although some psychologists prefer a more subjective, intuitive approach.

Before we venture forth into specific information about human habits and actions we should perhaps distinguish between psychology and psychiatry. The psychiatrist is a medically qualified person concerned with the diagnosis and treatment of mental illness and serious disorders of behaviour. The psychologist, on the other hand, is concerned with all aspects of behaviour, both the normal and the disturbed, and emphasizes the scientific methods in his search for knowledge.

Scientific method, which involves the systematic collection of data, and the testing of the description of that data, is universal. It is a systematization of common sense which involves logic and careful analysis of the processes of data-collecting and reasoning. Its application to a particular subject such as psychology leads to the development of specific techniques which are developed in terms of that subject. Four of the main techniques or methods employed by psychologists are : the experimental method; the natural observation method; the case history method; and the survey method.

The *experimental method*, sometimes called the laboratory method, is the one which most people associate with science, and it is by far the most important. Experiments are performed, usually in a laboratory, under carefully controlled conditions where precise, objective measurements can be carried out. Studies have been performed in the laboratory to find out about the structure of the nervous system, or the speed of reactions to lights, sounds, etc. Animal experiments are also made, as the principles of behaviour of animals can furnish useful clues about the nature of human behaviour. Many concepts of human learning were first suggested by clues gained through animal studies. Infant chimpanzees were found to 'prefer' a soft, cuddly form to a wire one, even though the latter contained the bottle which provided the only source of nourishment. (See Chapter 8.)

The laboratory conditions provide almost complete control

over the behaviour of the organism being studied, but these conditions also present one special difficulty. Behaviour that is shown in a laboratory may not be characteristic or representative of behaviour outside the laboratory. The very nature of the laboratory control presents an artificial environment which may distort the evidence in an unknown way. To resolve this problem, psychologists also study behaviour outside the laboratory.

In *natural observation* behaviour is examined in its natural setting. As much as possible, the psychologist tries to be unobtrusive, as he does not wish to have the same problems of artificiality that exist in the laboratory. By looking at behaviour as it happens in the natural environment he is more likely to obtain a true picture of how the individual behaves. (It is still possible to exercise some element of control, but this is typically done by special methods of statistical analysis which are too complicated to be considered in this book.) The natural observation method, like all the other methods described, is just one of the many that can be used to study an individual. A person may behave one way in the laboratory and somewhat differently outside, but if behaviour is studied under *both* conditions a more accurate set of data is obtained.

The *case history* is a somewhat different approach. Directed towards the past, it explores existing information and evidence of what has already happened. The rationale for this historical approach is simply that psychologists find that the best basis for predicting future behaviour is the evidence of past and present behaviour. Case history information is collected in many ways. The individual may be interviewed about his past, and school, employment, and other records are examined. Service records, accident reports, medical history information, and the comments of friends and neighbours are all pertinent sources of information.

The *survey method* differs from the others in that it is used to obtain information about group behaviour, collective attitudes, feelings, or habits, rather than about individual behaviour. We are, of course, all familiar with such opinion-gathering procedures as the Gallup Poll. The method that they use is the survey method, and their objective is to find out how a sample of people are inclined to act. From the data obtained from these samples, predictions can be made about how the population will act at a later date. Surveys help to discover what the public attitude is towards nationalization of industry, towards capital punishment, and even towards preferences of food and clothes. The survey method is extremely useful to psychologists working in business and industry.

A psychologist chooses his methods by examining the problem first and then selecting the technique which seems to be the most suitable. Thus a scientist interested in learning about the effects of noise from supersonic airliners would probably conduct studies in his laboratories with specially simulated sound effects. He would also visit the home areas of people subjected to noise and compare data obtained there with results found in the laboratory.

One of the new techniques that psychologists are using is the simulation of human processes by machines. Research workers in this field (which is known as cybernetics) have already programmed into machines, usually computers, some of the processes which appear to be involved in problem-solving and learning. By studying the problems of preparing the computer programmes, and then observing the operation of these machines, they have gained new insights into some aspects of human behaviour.

Forearmed with knowledge, the industrial psychologist can, among other things, help a company obtain the best workers and the clinical psychologist can better diagnose and treat his patient. Each is exercising some control over the actions of other people.

Summary

Psychology is the science which studies the behaviour of man and other animals. Four of the methods used are: the experimental method, the natural observation method, the case history method, and the survey method. The objectives for studying human behaviour are to understand, predict, and, in special cases, control human behaviour.

FURTHER READING

Hilgard, E. R., and Atkinson, R. C., *Introduction to Psychology* (4th edition), Methuen, 1966

Crow, L. D., and Crow, A., *Readings in General Psychology*, Constable, 1954

Pratt, C. C., *The Logic of Modern Psychology*, Macmillan, New York, 1939

CHAPTER TWO

SENSATION AND THE NERVOUS SYSTEM

OF all the features that distinguish man from animals, the most striking and the most complex is his ability to make sense to himself and to others of the world around him. He perceives, learns, thinks, remembers, and communicates in language and symbol to others. The general term used for the study of these abilities is cognition.

Through the senses we receive information about the world around us. We have at least eleven senses, but the five main ones are taste, touch, smell, hearing, and sight. Each of these senses supplies a different quality of information about our environment, but they normally work in harmony to give us a complex, multi-dimensional impression of the world. The brain is the control centre and the nerves resemble message lines, transmitting information from our senses to our brain.

There is a practical limit to the range of our senses. Taste is limited to the region of the mouth, touch to the limit of our arms. Smell has a greater range, yet is less sensitive in man than in other animals. Hearing has a much greater range than smelling; we can hear sounds that originate from great distances. Vision has the greatest range of all the senses, enabling us to see things as far off as the stars in the sky. Our sense of sight is also one of the more discriminating senses. A one-per-cent change in the brightness of the picture on our television

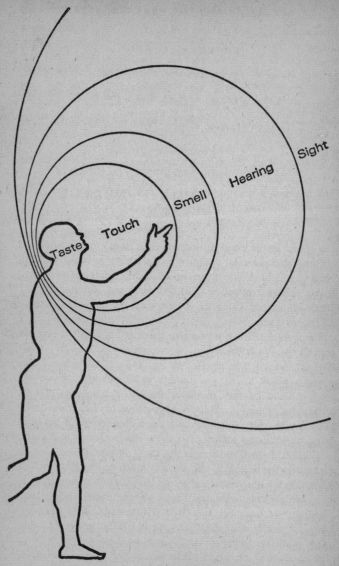

Taste　Touch　Smell　Hearing　Sight

Figure 1. Range of the senses

sets can be detected by the eye, but our ears must have a change of about ten per cent in the intensity of sound before any noticeable change is detected. Can you imagine what our feelings would be about our environment if our sense of touch, for example, were much more sensitive? Silk would feel like sandpaper. A down pillow could be mistaken for a bag of pine cones. If our ears were more sensitive the sound of breathing might be mistaken for a storm! Life would be drastically reorganized if our nose were as 'long' as our arm.

So far we have identified the five basic senses, but these are not the only means that man has for receiving information. The sense of touch, for example, can be divided into four separate sub-senses of pressure, pain, warmth, and cold. Each has its characteristic receptors, and there are varying concentrations of the receptors in the body. The ends of the fingers have a large number of pressure receptors, but the back of the hand has very few. Additional senses include the 'sense of balance', governed by the operation of a set of semi-circular canals in the ear. The eye also gives us cues to balance, as does our sense of touch, but the ear canals are the main organs for equilibrium. Travel sickness occurs when the ear canals are over-stimulated; the pills that people take to relieve these symptoms are intended to reduce the sensitivity of these organs.

Further body senses include the sense of hunger and thirst, and the sense of body movement. We can walk from place to place because of the automatic nature of our body sense. If we concentrate on each step, we trip over our own feet. The sense of body movement, called the kinaesthetic sense, also tells us our position in space. You could, for example, touch the end of your nose, with your eyes closed, without any other cues or direction. The guidance system by which your finger finds the location of your nose is the way the kinaesthetic sense operates. Kinaesthesis is a sort of muscle sense.

Already we have listed at least eleven senses of man without any mention of such concepts as the sense of music or art, which are complicated combinations of the others rather than unitary or primary senses. All the senses listed are inborn instruments for obtaining information about our surroundings, and all of them, for most people, go into working order within a few months after birth.

Each sense organ responds to energy (the ear to sound energy, the eye to light waves, etc.) which it transforms into nerve impulses. These nerve impulses are sent along nerve fibres in the nervous system to the brain. The nervous system is an intricate set of fibres. There are different pathways for different types of messages. The sensory (afferent) nerve cells and fibres pick up their information from the sense organs and transmit the messages to the spinal cord, which acts as the 'trunk line' for messages to the brain. Messages coming down from the brain are called motor (efferent) impulses and are directed to the muscles which go into action in response to these messages. Although scientists have been able to discover this specialization of the different nerve fibres, they still have a great deal to learn about the nature of nerve 'messages' and how they are coded and dealt with by the brain.

Various different areas of the brain specialize in the receipt and translation of the nerve impulses arriving from particular sense organs. The back portion of the cerebrum receives the nerve impulses from the eyes. The top portion takes in the touch senses. The brain, of course, performs many functions not clearly understood by psychologists and neurologists. Apparently, the brain receives and sorts the messages, and those that are of little or no use to the person are filtered out. The multitude of noises, sounds, smells that are always around us are banished, preventing our internal message centres from being clogged up with irrelevant or distracting information. These messages that are useful or important are sorted and translated. Imagine yourself behind the wheel of your car, when suddenly the traffic lights turn red. The red traffic light will be transmitted through the eye, stimulating nerve impulses to the brain. A return message from the brain activates your leg which depresses the brake pedal so that the car stops at the cross-roads. Other light stimuli, such as the colour of the sky, other cars, shop windows, people, will also be transmitted through your sense of sight but the brain will filter them out as being irrelevant to your needs at that moment. It is not known how much of this information is stored away in the brain as a permanent record but it is certain that the brain has an enormous capacity for storage. If we tried to build a computer to perform all of the functions of the human brain it would probably have to be large enough to fill many classrooms in a university. Yet man's brain is squeezed into a cavity at the top of the head, filling a space smaller than

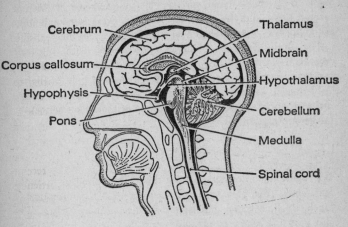

Figure 2. The brain

the size of his hat. With about ten thousand million interconnected cells the brain can receive, sort, analyse, and store an enormous amount of material for future reference. The brain is the source of thought, reason, imagination, complex learning, problem-solving, and other 'high-level' activities. As a co-ordination and control centre it has the admiration of the most advanced engineer. Modern electronic computers can operate faster than the human brain, making a few thousand calculations in the interval of an eye blink, but as they are normally used they lack the versatility of the human brain. On the other hand, computers can now be programmed to show an increasingly high percentage of that versatility, and it is reasonable to suppose that eventually a computer will perform the full range of human acts.

It is a popular misunderstanding that the difference between intelligent, talented people and the less intelligent ones is due to a difference in the size of the brain or the number of cells. Careful research has disproved this theory. One of the largest brains ever found came from a mentally defective person. The difference between qualities and quantities of mental ability seems to be related to the way in which the cells are connected to each other and the way they function. This subject is one of the frontiers of knowledge that scientists are exploring.

The brain has also complex associations with internal emotional alarm systems, by way of the thalamus and hypothalamus, which activate emergency responses of fight or flight.

The brain, in short, can be thought of as a complicated control and storage system which depends primarily on sensation for its information.

Summary

We receive our information about the world around us through our senses. We have at least eleven senses, including taste, touch, smell, hearing, and sight: the five primary senses. We also have the senses of pressure, pain, heat, cold, hunger and thirst, balance, and body sense. The sensory information is transmitted along nerve pathways to the brain where messages that are important are used, the unimportant is filtered away.

FURTHER READING

Geldard, F. A., *The Human Senses*, New York and London, Wiley, 1953

Morgan, C. T., and Stellar, E., *Physiological Psychology* (2nd edition), New York and London, McGraw-Hill, 1950

CHAPTER THREE

PERCEPTION

WHAT we sense we interpret, and this psychological process is called 'perception'. As Chapter 2 made clear, this takes place in the brain. The brain is also sorting and filtering a wealth of stimuli, most of which we are neither aware of, nor do we interpret; but by perception we mean the process by which we *become aware* of and *interpret* or identify the sensations we receive. There are a multitude of factors that influence our perceptions. Inheritance seems to be one factor. Depth perception, for example, is a response that is found in very young children, and also in new-born animals. (See plate 2.) Learning is another influence. The native Londoner perceives a sunny day with a temperature of 75° F. as hot and oppressive. In a place near the Equator, however, he might feel this same set of conditions to be a pleasant change from more uncomfortable higher temperatures. In much the same way, people who have lived with central heating for a year or two find a warm house very comfortable. Their neighbours may regard the warm air in the same house as confining and uncomfortable. Perception depends on what you are used to, what you expect, and the context of your experience. In all of these illustrations, the interpretation placed upon the degree of comfort is, above all, a matter of what the person has experienced and learned in the past.

Our learning experiences also help us to understand the differences in the sensations we receive. If we look at a car coming down the road towards us, it seems to become larger and larger : that is to say, the images on our eyes are successively larger. Now one, admittedly unlikely, interpretation of this is that the car is not really moving at all, but is expanding. Either type of event, a car moving towards us or its being stationary and expanding, would give us the *same* visual sensation. But our previous experience tells us that a car is bearing down upon us, and if we wish to survive we had better leap out of the way; inappropriate perceptual interpretation may sometimes prove fatal to survival. The same impression, or perception, can be created by wholly different sources of information.

Inheritance and experience are not the only factors which affect our understanding of the stimuli from our senses. All the different cues about the stimulus will determine the way we interpret it. A car approaching us will not only become larger, but it will also noticeably reduce the amount of road that remains visible. This change in information that our eye receives is another cue for our understanding of what is going on. The surrounding cues and features of the environment, derivable from all our different senses, collectively, contribute to the total process of perception. They may aid or distort our knowledge of our world.

Consider the two lines in the figure below and decide which is the longer.

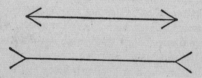

The top one with the arrow ends seems to be shorter, but if you measure them you will find them to be exactly the same in length. This illustrates that the *total context* of an object we are observing may change our perception of it. This relation between the stimulus-in-the-context and the viewer causes the perception to be incorrect. This sort of phenomenon is sometimes called a visual illusion. It is a distortion of reality that almost all people experience. The movement of the pictures of the cinema, where the still pictures are successively exposed to the eye to give the effect of movement, is also, in an obvious sense, illusory. Even more obvious is the impression of movement created by successive 'still pictures' which are 'flicked over' quickly by hand. The impression of movement depends, of course, on the continuity between successive pictures.

The brain sorts out all the information from all our senses and in some way integrates it so that we perceive accurately. If, for example, we see a person hit a ball with a cricket bat and the ball speeds away to the boundary we would regard it as a familiar experience that is readily understood. If we heard no sound when the bat met the ball we would wonder how to account for this unusual experience and would probably guess that a soft ball rather than the ordinary hard ball was being used. Much of our understanding of what our combined sensations perceive depends upon the simultaneous occurrence of events. Our ideas about cause and effect indeed are based upon the simultaneous occurrence of sensations of stimuli which occur in a particular order, wherein, for example, the sound of the bat hitting the ball must not precede the sight of the bat hitting the ball.

Another type of influence upon perception is the condition or state of the person at the time. We *tend to perceive things as we need or want to be rather than as they are*. Standing on the street corner and waiting for someone we know, we find that we may make a number of errors of recognition. We think a person is our friend, and he is a complete stranger. This tendency to interpret things or people in a way that satisfies our motives or needs is typical of the manner in which our mental processes operate in perception. The reverse can also happen. We may not notice someone we are very familiar with, simply because we are not expecting to meet him. A thirsty man in the desert may perceive the heat waves and other stimuli in the distance as sources of water. The person on a diet, depriving himself of food, will take notice of many more edible things than people eating normally; ambiguous stimuli, like clouds, begin to look like food objects.

The processes of perception are complex and apply to the whole range of sensations. The field of visual perception happens to be the one which has been most frequently investigated and therefore most usefully discussed.

We tend to divide the visual world up into *figure* and *ground*, and although generally the figure protrudes from the ground and stands out prominently, this is not always or necessarily the case. The very fact of dividing the visual world into figure and ground leads to a new sort of visual illusion, or rather what is called an ambiguous figure. There are many examples of ambiguous figures, for example a transparent cube. This may be perceived, in any one position, as seen from either below or above. It may also be perceived as a flat two-dimensional figure, and indeed there may be no limit to the possible interpretations of such a sensory stimulus.

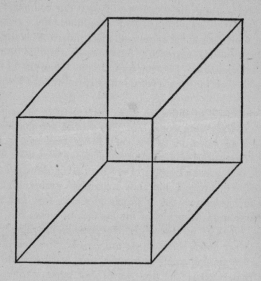

There are many further experiments in perception which show the complicated interrelated nature of the process. One is the distorted room which looks normal from one angle but is in fact distorted so that two men of equal size standing in opposite corners of the room look like a giant and a midget respectively. (See plate 1.)

Another example is that of a trapezoidal window that appears to oscillate when it is actually rotating at a steady velocity. Another example is that of lighted disks. If we see two lighted disks, where one is brighter than the other the brighter one looks nearer; or if it is larger rather than brighter it still looks nearer; and if it is both brighter and larger it looks very much the nearer of the two, even though in all cases it is in fact the same distance from the observer. These examples, and there are many more, emphasize the complex processes involved in the way we, as human beings, interpret our surroundings.

Finally E.S.P. (to dispose of any possible misconceptions) is a subject little related to the study of visual perception. The words 'extra-sensory perception' imply the possibility of acquiring information through some means other than the ordinary sensory channels. The use of words such as 'extra-sensory perception' seems, of course, to be self-contradictory, but what is implied is that all information is not necessarily carried through the *known* senses, and of the experiments that have been carried out, one typical one is that of selecting a series of playing cards at one place which a person many miles away has been able to predict with an accuracy that cannot be accounted for easily by the laws of chance. A number of experiments have been carried out which suggest the possibility of such communication, but no definite evidence is yet available as to whether it actually takes place.

Summary

Perception is the process by which we become aware of and interpret our sensations about the world around us. There are many different factors that influence our perceptions, such as the cues from the stimulus, the surroundings, the experiences we have derived from the past, the inherited abilities we were born with, and finally the many different motives, needs, and desires at the moment of the perception.

FURTHER READING

Boring, E. G., *Sensation and Perception in the History of Experimental Psychology, Mayflower*, 1942

Gibson, J. J., *The Perception of the Visual World*, Boston, Houghton Mifflin, 1950 (London, Allen & Unwin, 1952)

Vernon, M. D., *A further Analysis of Perception*, Cambridge University Press, 1954

CHAPTER FOUR

MOTIVATION

We are born with certain fundamental needs or drives which cause us to behave in ways tending to ensure our physical survival. These basic drives are those which lead us to seek warmth, protection, the satisfaction of hunger and thirst, and the avoidance of pain and suffocation, and which maintain all the biological processes needed for survival. As we grow up, other motives are acquired through learning and personal experience. If we are treated with tender, loving care during our infancy we will learn that association with other people is a source of pleasure. Accordingly, we are likely to enjoy the company of others as we get older. Many of our adult motives for behaviour can be traced back to the early learning experiences in childhood when many experiences are associated with the satisfaction of basic needs. These experiences produce secondary motives, some of which gain strength and persistence. Acquired motives can be divided into two categories: common social motives and common personal motives.

The common social needs listed below have been observed as motives of behaviour among people from many different societies and cultures. The needs are:

RECOGNITION:

Most people want praise and credit for their efforts and accomplishments, i.e. they want to be recognized for what they think they are, and this may involve the use of the 'club' badge in one form or another.

ACCEPTANCE:

Many people require a feeling of belonging, in which other people regard them as trustworthy and worthwhile individuals. The clubs we join, the friends we associate with, etc., all often satisfy our desire for acceptance.

INDEPENDENCE:

Many people have a need to exercise some control over their
affairs and to feel free and independent. Some individuals attain
this feeling simply by dressing differently although such behaviour can conflict with the desire for acceptance and group
membership. Independence-needs may be satisfied in part by
opportunities to suggest ideas and to participate with others in
the making of decisions. The need may also be satisfied if the
mere opportunity to control and influence our affairs is available, even if it is not taken.

SECURITY:

Many people have varying needs for security, which may be ful-
filled in different ways. To one person, security means the accumulation of savings, and other needs are subordinated to this
goal. To some, security means a permanent job or a happy
home. Like all the other motives we have described security is
a relative thing. The manual worker who is working only a
few days a week may feel quite secure; but another employee,
in the same situation, may feel very insecure.

Although one could go on adding to this list of common
social motives it is worth bearing in mind that the way we behave is largely a matter of our perceptions of our environment
and our learned motives. If we feel that we are deprived of the
satisfactions associated with any of these motives we are more
likely to be galvanized into action. The direction and the degree
of success of our efforts will be governed by the choices for
satisfaction available, as well as the learned habitual patterns for
pursuing the goal.

In addition to the basic drives and the social needs which
activate and direct our behaviour, there is also a large collection
of motives in the category of personal needs. The personal
motives are those that drive us to fulfil our ideas of our self as a
person. These self-achievement motives include the desire to
'maintain one's good name', to acquire material or 'spiritual'
possessions, to dominate other people, to invent things, or to do

virtually anything which will give us a sense of attainment and self-respect.

When we are hungry we may purchase our food or steal it. Even under extreme hunger, however, we may refrain from stealing: the need for freedom can take precedence over basic motives. The constellation of our personal motives and our individual patterns for their achievement and satisfaction are marks which distinguish each of us as unique, individual personalities.

Although the motives of human behaviour have been listed here in such a way that they may seem to be clear-cut concepts that are easily identified, the contrary is true. The causes of our behaviour are intertwined into a complicated set of drives and motives and the combination of motives that initiates any particular act we commit may be determined by any one of a multitude of possible causes. The combinations of motives that are driving us may be as inexhaustible as the number of ways a pools coupon may be written.

Our motives are of course not randomly mixed but align themselves according to a number of influences. One of these processes of setting up motivational priorities is as follows. If we have been without food for a long period of time, our hunger drive may be dominant. Immediately after eating, the hunger need decreases in strength and immediacy. As time passes, the need for food will rise again in intensity and become more and more influential upon our behaviour. All our motives are in a state of flux. They successively pull us towards different avenues of satisfaction and remove the sense of need after they are satisfied. The process of satisfaction itself is a process which essentially involves the giving of pleasure or the removal of pain.

The motives we have do not appear as direct causes of behaviour but may be disguised and obscure. Consider three men in a pub, each drinking a glass of beer. One man may simply be satisfying a thirst drive. The second man may be in the pub in search of others to associate with and thereby satisfy his social needs for acceptance and recognition. The third man, suffering from a variety of personal problems, may be trying to drown his sorrows in the vague hope of recovering his self-esteem. All three are apparently behaving the same way, and yet each is achieving the satisfaction of a different need. This shows that different motives may be satisfied by what appears as the same kind of behaviour. On the other hand, one motive may lead to many different forms and expressions of behaviour. For one thirsty man, the half-pint at the pub is sufficient. To another thirsty man, many cups of tea is the only source of satisfaction. To a third, sucking on a mint, which activates the salivary glands, may satisfy him. This shows different behaviour springing from the same motive. This may be an obvious example, but the implications are far-reaching. It may often be quite difficult to decide on the different motives that drive people to different sorts of behaviour. Motivational research is a branch of psychology concerned precisely with this sort of analysis.

Our motives, which we have called primary, are basic to survival. Through experience we acquire social and other secondary motives. These secondary motives vary for different people and motivational analysis or research tries to unravel the associations which have occurred in different individuals. These associations help to determine and direct our day-to-day behaviour.

We must also remember that we are often motivated by impulses that we are not aware of. These unconscious motives seem to govern much of our activity. We cannot often say with accuracy why we did this or that, and not the other.

As we said earlier, we learn how to satisfy our needs and also develop needs through the learning process. This capacity to modify and change our responses and not to respond to inborn or instinctive drives only is one of the characteristics which distinguish humans from other living creatures and from most machines. The plasticity or flexibility of behaviour is the way we develop what is called *purpose* in life. All motives are purposeful, but where the basic drives satisfy the objective of survival, other experiences associated with that satisfaction may become needs and motives themselves quite independent of their original association. The young child who has to fight for his nourishment may grow up to be an aggressive person, as if the threat of hunger was always present in his environment. He may generalize this aggression towards the entire social structure in which he lives, and not only will he grab for his food, but for everything else that might be within reach. When he becomes an adult this reaction could be transferred to the desire for job promotion, a position in a queue, or any other objective which gives him the sense of satisfaction. A motivated behaviour, once rooted in childhood conditions, may later become independent of its cause and yet the response may persist. Quite clearly, the desire to perform some sort of action, or even become some sort of person in society, will depend upon the associations that have been acquired in the past. The result of the experiences of the home and the school can motivate a young person against a particular way of life if the experiences were painful. Experiences which are associated with pleasure will tend to motivate a person in favour of that way of life; however, other forces or factors may intervene.

The sex motive is a complicated drive or motive, and there is no general agreement about it. The Freudian theory supports the idea that sex drives are part of the basic motives and are fundamental to our survival and well-being. Other theorists, notably the behaviourists, counter with the fact that people such as unmarried clergymen, bachelors, etc., live long useful lives and are apparently happy. Some people can subordinate the sex drive to an acquired goal. The need for sexual satisfaction probably comes after the survival needs in the hierarchy of personal and social needs.

The conflict between motives like the need for sex and the need for food was reported in a study of nutrition performed some years ago. A group of scientists were engaged to study the effects of limited, minimum diets upon military personnel. A group of naval volunteers were selected and placed in an isolated camp where they were given special foods, and were kept under close supervision. These subjects also did work on the base but were not allowed to leave the grounds while the experiment was being conducted. One of the sidelights which came out of this study was the report that the men no longer dreamt of girls at night, but instead mainly about food. They dreamt about food in all forms, and in large quantities. Their behaviour also changed accordingly. They removed pin-up pictures from their walls and replaced them with pictures of food dishes obtained from magazines. At the end of the study, when the men were returned to normal diets and allowed to leave the base to satisfy all of their motives, the food pictures came down and the female pictures returned. This isolated study is not offered as conclusive proof of the dominance of the food drive over the sex drive. However, other studies conducted under rigorous, controlled laboratory conditions substantiate the results obtained from the study of the 'hungry' males.

'Homeostasis' is the name given to the stabilizing process whereby a need sets up a type of behaviour which ceases when the need is satisfied. The organism is like a homeostatic system which seeks out satisfactions and avoids dangers in an attempt to keep itself in a stable state.

Homeostasis in organisms is much like the operation of a servo system, which is an automatic control system. When a homeostat is used to control the domestic water supply, for example (when, of course, it is called a 'thermostat'), then it switches on the heat when the water reaches a lower temperature and switches it off when it reaches an upper temperature. This is a simple example of the process of need-satisfaction and drive-reduction which is the core of the whole motivational process.

Summary

Motivation activates and directs our behaviour. It is a driving force shaping action into purposeful activity. The motives may be divided into the survival motives which satisfy bodily needs, the social motives which satisfy needs for success among people, and our personal needs which achieve our desire for self-esteem. These motives are in flux, are disguised, and are difficult to connect directly to any single act. One motive may initiate many different forms of behaviour, and many motives may result in the same form of behaviour. Our motives, needs, and drives are influenced by learning and are intimately related to our search for gratification.

FURTHER READING

Tyler, L. E., *The Psychology of Human Differences* (2nd edition), New York, Appleton-Century-Crofts, 1956 (London, Mayflower)

CHAPTER FIVE

SIMPLE LEARNING

LEARNING is a process with which we are all familiar. We have experienced it at home, at school, on the playing fields, and at work. In fact, learning has probably taken place in virtually every activity in which we have taken part. *Learning* may be defined, rather generally, as *changes in behaviour as the result of past experience*. It has sometimes been called 'habit formation', but that only depicts one aspect of the complicated nature of learning.

Psychologists have formulated a number of theories about how learning takes place and have performed a great deal of research with humans and animals in an attempt to gain a better understanding of the process. Theories have been proposed by Pavlov, Skinner, Thorndike, Köhler, and Hull, to name but a few leading psychologists. We shall try to relate some of these theories to daily behaviour.

One of the most important studies of learning, like many great discoveries of science, was initiated almost by accident. At the beginning of this century a Russian physiologist named Ivan Pavlov was continuing his research on the reflex processes associated with digestion. While observing the behaviour of the dogs on which he was working as laboratory subjects, he noticed that the flow of saliva in the mouth occurred *not only* when food was placed in the dog's mouth but even *before*, at the sight of the food. The dog's responses to the food in the mouth were considered automatic reflex responses that are inborn, but the response to the *sight* of the food was a learned, or conditioned, response. Pavlov re-directed his efforts to explore this response.

He found that the dogs could be taught to react the same way (by salivating) not only to the sight of food but to the sound of a bell, the ticking of a metronome, or even the rotating motion of a disk. Ringing the 'dinner bell', or using any other signal that the dog associated with the food, would cause the animal to respond in almost the same way as if the food was placed directly into his mouth. He accounted for the learning process according to the following sequence of events:

First: a stimulus applied, such as a bell being rung;
immediately after: meat placed in the dog's mouth;
reaction: the dog responded by salivating.

By repeating this sequence a number of times, the dog would now salivate when the bell alone was sounded. The sequence of signal–food–response became:

signal–response

The food was called the unconditioned stimulus, as it was a stimulus that caused an automatic, reflexive, unconditioned response. The signal, which was the sight of the food or a bell, was called the conditioned stimulus, and the response to the signal, the conditioned response. The distinction was made between the 'natural' (unconditioned) response to the food and the learned (conditioned) response, as they were not *exactly* the same. The learned response seemed to be more complicated, as the dogs also acted with an air of expectancy and uncertainty whenever the signal alone was made. This signal–response sequence for learning is called 'classical conditioning'.

There is a widespread feeling that all learning is built up by the same process of association of such symbols or signs in close relationship with the things they symbolize or signify. Added evidence for this viewpoint is supplied by studies on higher-order conditioning. Second-order conditioning, for example, is accomplished in approximately the following manner. The animal or person is first conditioned to respond to a signal like a bell in the way described above. The original signal is now paired with another signal like a light. The training sequence is:

light–bell–response.

Again, after a suitable number of such combinations, the subject will now respond to the light as he did to the bell. The habit of responding to the signal can be strengthened by only an occasional presentation of the food or unconditioned stimulus. Further higher-order associations can be made by pairing a word with the light, and so on. This is a gradual process of building up the learning of associations that link together many different signals or stimuli.

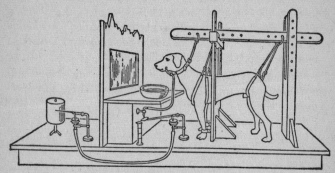

Figure 3. Collection of saliva in Pavlov's early experiments

Just as in the original experiments the signals became associated with the food by their close association, that association can be extinguished by reversing the procedure. If the bell is sounded frequently and the food is never presented, the salivation response will gradually diminish and eventually stop. After a while, however, the bell will be found still to cause the original conditioned response although it had seemed to be extinguished. Further 'bell without food' pairings are necessary before the response is completely eliminated. The organism generally takes longer to 'unlearn' the response than it did to learn it. How many people have a fright reaction whenever a siren like an air-raid warning is sounded? Conditioned responses, once acquired, are very tenacious, and it may be a long time before all traces can be eliminated.

Many psychologists took up the study of this scheme of learning after 1904 when Pavlov was awarded a Nobel Prize in Medicine for his work on the digestive processes. We have space here only to point out that some of our behaviour patterns are probably developed through such signal–response associations. Signals like the dinner bell, the sight of food, the names or symbols of things like juicy steaks or appetizing dinners, are enough to elicit the responses of salivation we have been conditioned to.

It is important to mention that we may learn to avoid certain signals, signs, or symbols just as we can be conditioned to respond positively towards others. If a child is presented with a fuzzy, black bear as a toy, but is suddenly startled, perhaps by a loud noise, at the same moment as the toy is offered, that child might very likely be frightened every time that toy is offered to him. Only after many trials where the toy is presented and the startling noise or stimulus is absent will the child cease to be afraid. This fear-provoking toy can become a generalized signal for a disturbance, and the child can be frightened not only by that fuzzy bear but even by other fuzzy objects, or even beards, if they are perceived by him as having the property of fuzziness.

A different type of learning, sometimes called operant conditioning, was described more recently by B. F. Skinner of Harvard University. He examined the way learning takes place when the behaviour is spontaneous and not at the reflex level, as it is in classical conditioning. Skinner constructed a box which has inside it a lever that can be operated, a food tray, and a buzzer. When a typically hungry animal is placed inside this box it normally wanders around since its desire for food activates it. In this searching, random behaviour, the animal may accidentally depress the lever. This lever operates a machine that delivers food in the form of pellets that drop into a tray. When the animal finds the pellets he is likely to continue his explorations and will very likely depress the lever again, and be rewarded with further food pellets which again will be consumed. After a short time, and after a number of rewards or reinforcements like this, the animal learns to press away in order to obtain food. It will work and consume the food until it has had enough. This learning scheme, where the animal operates a lever to satisfy his need, is essentially :

response–reward.

We should notice that the reward, or as it is usually called in psychology the 'reinforcement', comes after the response has been made. Also, the first correct response occurs almost purely by chance. In classical conditioning, by contrast, the food reward came before and the automatic response followed on. Both operant conditioning (which is Skinner's term for this sort of conditioning) and classical conditioning are association schemes: classical conditioning being an association between a signal and a response; operant conditioning being an association between a response and a reward. The first method is connected with automatic, reflective types of response; the latter type seems to be connected with voluntary modes of action and behaviour.

We mentioned earlier that the Skinner box had a buzzer connected to it but it was not employed. If we change the situation now so that this buzzer is connected with the food machine so that it sounds each time the lever is depressed, and the animal receives a food reward, the buzzer will seem to take on the same rewarding qualities or associations that were also attached to the food. When the well-fed animal is later put back in the box it will push the lever a few times, as if it is a result of a pleasantly familiar past activity, and then it will ignore it. If, however, the buzzer sounds with each press of the lever, the animal will press many times, as the buzzer seems to be its own reward. The behaviour which is elicited for the buzzer 'reward' alone seems to be a *secondary reinforcement*. If we now wish to teach this animal another kind of response, such as the pressing of a button, all that has to be done is to connect up the button with the buzzer. When the button is pressed for the first time accidentally, the buzzer will sound. Thereafter we can observe the development of this new response to the secondary reinforcement. Third-order associations, and even higher ones, can be developed in this way.

How do we develop the many complex chains of habits that we make? They are probably learned by a combination of the two learning conditions, i.e.:

    (a) *Signal–response*

and (b) *Response–reward*, thus

      Signal–response–reward.

Thorndike's Law of Effect summarizes this course of events. It states that satisfying experiences tend to be repeated when the organism can bring it about. Also, painful states are avoided whenever possible. The reward may be a pleasurable or need-satisfying experience, or it may be some event that is an avoidance of punishment. These signals, which were paired with, or associated with, rewards that originally satisfied our motives or needs, later tend to take on their own reinforcing qualities. Like the buzzer in the Skinner box, we may behave as if we are trying to achieve rewards that are actually well satisfied, but the associations with them are the higher-order rewards that we now prefer.

A special machine, known as the Chimpomat, has been used in studies of chimps to teach them to work for grapes. Poker chips were substituted for the grapes in the pay-off mechanism. The chips could then be deposited in the machine and grapes delivered. It was then found that the chimps would work for poker chips and save a few before they converted them.

The chip had acquired value like money. The poker chips may have acquired rewarding qualities that are quite independent of the pleasant memories associated with the time when these were capable of being exchanged for food. Other signs or symbols likewise acquire their meaning, in part, from the objects or events they were associated with.

It has been known for a long time that human memory is associative. One thing reminds us of another for various reasons – either they occurred together originally, or they refer to the same subject matter in some sense. Human learning is only partly a matter of association of responses acquired through classical or operant conditioning experiences. Our acquired behaviour seems to be too complex to be exclusively accounted for by these two types of causes.

Trial-and-error is an approach to the solving of problems and the search for ways to satisfy motives. Trial-and-error is the beginning of a process that soon becomes non-random. W. Köhler, a German psychologist who worked in America, demonstrated the important role of a non-random scheme for learning, called 'insight'. We mean by 'insight' the solution of a new problem by combining previously learned experiences or solutions to problems in a new way. It is the formation of a new association for the organism trying to solve a problem – or reach a goal.

Köhler arranged for a chimpanzee to be placed in a room which had a banana suspended from the ceiling. Scattered around the room were a number of packing boxes. The chimp normally would try to get the banana by leaping up, but the food was too high for him. After what would appear to be useless pauses and much fretting, the animal would suddenly act as if he healized the solution. He would leap into action, piling the boxes one on top of the other, until the pile was high enough to allow the chimpanzee to climb up and get the reward. (See Pate 3b.)

In this and many other such problems the chimpanzees acted *as if* they developed an understanding of the behaviour necessary for the solution of the problem. In later studies it was clear that this type of problem-solving would not take place if the animal had not had previous experiences with boxes. In effect, for this problem to be solved, an old response (experience) had to be applied in a new way, through insight. Learning to solve problems by remembering and using previous experiences in this way is very much a human method for achieving our goals and objectives. If the new problem is important to us, then our achievement of the solution may be very rewarding indeed.

We can summarize the findings of this chapter by pointing out that all the different forms of learning have some element of association in them, and some element of reinforcement. Thorndike's Law of Effect accounts for this course of events, although learning may sometimes seem much more complicated than these conditioning schemes would suggest.

Summary

Learning is any change in behaviour that results from past experience, if we exclude, of course, such artificial cases as injuries and the like. The different learning schemes described included classical conditioning or signal–response learning; operant conditioning or response–reward learning; insight learning; and others. Our habit patterns of behaviour are probably developed from a combination of these arrangements, and they can be generally accounted for by the consequences of the Law of Effect.

FURTHER READING

Broadhurst, P. L., *The Science of Animal Behaviour*, Penguin, 1963
Hilgard, E. R., and Bower, G. H., *Theories of Learning* (3rd edition), Methuen, 1966

CHAPTER SIX

COMPLEX LEARNING AND LANGUAGE

THE basic principle of learning, as we saw in the last chapter, is reinforcement. When the student or learner does something that leads to success he is much more likely to repeat it; when he fails, he is not likely to repeat it. The reinforcements do not necessarily have to occur every time the pupil responds. There is a wealth of evidence to show that occasional, or partial, reinforcement can sometimes be even more effective than constant reinforcement. The reinforcement can be either reward or avoidance of threatened punishment. It is preferable to learn under the incentive of rewards rather than the threat of punishments.

Some degree of motivation (drives or needs mean something very similar) is also essential to efficient learning. Human beings can sometimes acquire knowledge without deliberate effort, but the results are limited. For example, as passengers in a car, we may take little or no notice of the route travelled. If, however, we must now guide the driver on the return journey, we discover that we had in fact acquired quite a lot of information about the route taken. This type of learning, which occurs without intention or obvious cause, is called *latent learning*. One definition of it is: 'any learning which is not immediately manifested in performance'.

The only way we can be sure that learning has taken place is if it is manifested in performance. The performance is brought forth usually under the offer of some sort of reward which the individual is motivated to acquire. To put the matter simply though, we may say that we learn better if we *want* or *need* to learn.

Many different kinds of conditions of motivation affect the way we learn. If we are trying to teach someone a lesson, his desire to learn will enhance his achievement; but too much motivation can lead to extreme anxiety and excitement which will actually interfere with the learning process. Moderate, not intense, desire is needed. External rewards such as money, or even marks for classroom work in a school, will be effective only if they are what the student wants. If these particular incentives are not important to him they may fail. Not only must the reward be desired, but the material to be learned must also have *meaning*.

Another vital condition of learning is that the student knows how he is performing. If you were to practise throwing darts blindfolded, you might build up the arm muscles but there would be no improvement in learning or performance. If, however, you take notice of the information that comes to your senses, and perceive it appropriately, then this so-called *feedback* will allow you to correct your mistakes in turn, and then with practice you can go on to develop your skill.

Another important consideration, especially in the development of skills and performance, is distribution. Distribution of learning and practice allows the material or skill to be much better assimilated. Imagine the success of a person who tries to learn the piano by practising for ten successive hours. His learning will be much more effective if this effort is spread, say, over a ten-day period with only one hour each day.

Just as excessive motivation interferes with success, so does over-concentrated practice. Study and learning for examinations, for example, should be spread over the entire term and not crammed into the few days before the test. This is not to say that cramming will be ineffective. The performance upon which the student is evaluated is the one he delivers on examination day. If 'cramming' helps him for that day, then he should do it. If, however, he wants to retain the material and make a more permanent gain in learning, then that learning should be acquired over a longer period.

Transfer of training is another very important concept: what has been learned in one situation can be used in other situations. A person who has learned to drive one model of car is normally able to learn to drive another model quickly. This enhanced learning experience is called *positive transfer*. Yet at the same time, interference may also occur when you learn to operate the second car. The similarity of the two situations may mislead you into some responses which are now quite inappropriate. Imagine, for example, the way you would give hand-signals in the left-hand drive car. Having previously learned to signal with the right hand, the first efforts in the new situation might cause you to wave your right hand under the nose of your passenger in the front seat, rather than make the correct signals with the left hand. This interference in effective performance, called *negative transfer*, is accentuated by the similarity in the situation. The question of whether previous experience will enhance or interfere with future learning is a question of what skills are required and whether they are augmented in the new situation or must first be unlearned.

Complex human learning is a process of many associations in knowledge, skills, and attitudes. We must also be able to generalize from these associations and apply them in novel situations.

Let us look at a familiar and simple problem in arithmetic: what is the sum of 1 and 1? The learning of the correct association leads to the answer, 2. This answer is developed, perhaps, according to the various principles outlined. The object of teaching a person to achieve the one and only correct association according to prescribed rules of arithmetic is called the teaching of convergent or deductive thinking. Our understanding of what the symbols in a mathematics problem mean and the relationship those symbols have to each other obviously leads us to respond with the correct association according to the prescribed rules, so $1 + 1 = 2$.

Convergent thinking is not the only kind that we use, or should use, to solve problems. We also must be able to give to a new problem new, imaginative, and creative answers, which might be better solutions. This is essentially the inductive as opposed to the deductive process. What else can the supposed combination of the symbol 1 and another 1 make? What about 11, or 7, or T, or V, or L, or X, or any other meaningful combination? Any of these combinations of the two symbols *might* be useful answers arrived at by creative or divergent thinking, although they do not, of course, make any mathematical sense.

We are taught, to some small degree, both kinds of thinking at school, but it is often thought that we should master the more conventional or convergent methods before we can experiment with novel and divergent methods.

Imagination enables us to free our thinking from the rules of axiomatic systems to an open-minded, creative treatment of problems. If we can manage to generate new associations to a problem (11, 7, T, V, L, X), we must also evaluate each one for appropriateness. The right answer is the new association that is appropriate to the problem, and that association only. Creative thinking is successful only if the individual is able both to associate and evaluate effectively.

The distinction we have made between convergent (regulative) thinking and divergent (imaginative) thinking is, as we have mentioned, much the same as the difference between *deduction* and *induction*.

Deduction may take place in ordinary language, so we say that 'if I am in Bath and Bath is in Somerset', then 'I am in Somerset'. We can, of course, construct more formal systems wherein we can deduce that given AB (i.e. A implies B) and given BC, then we can say AC merely on account of the rules of the system.

Inductive thinking now supplies the basis (the axioms) from

which deductions are made. It is the setting-up of the inductive basis of argument that is essentially the creative or imaginative process. 'If all ducks waddle, then the next duck I see will waddle.' This is a reasonable deductive inference, leaving the question as to whether or not all ducks waddle. This is not something that can be shown to be universally true, but the very fact of conjoining the properties of being a duck and waddling is essentially the creative act, however obvious and simple in this case.

One may guess that there is only a small step from such imaginative and logical arguments as that just quoted to a consideration of language. We have mentioned symbol training, where, for example, we learn to use symbols to represent or symbolize. If we take this one step further we have language, where statements refer to events and their relation to each other.

Language is a major factor in complex learning. Human beings learn a great deal about the world by merely observing and recording information. This is sometimes called *learning by acquaintance*. They also learn by verbal description, and this means that we do not have to go to France to know that France exists. Indeed the bulk of human knowledge depends upon knowledge *learned by description*.

The most complex features of learning, the beginnings of which may be seen in symbol learning in chimpanzees, are dependent upon the ability to formulate problems in language and to argue logically and with insight in terms of language. We shall now deal with a brief study of language for the rest of this chapter.

Semantics

It is not easy to define 'semantics' precisely, partly because the word has been used in more than one way. But we can say that it is always concerned with the *meaning* of words and sentences. In fact, it could be concerned with the meaning of any sort of *signs* or symbols whatever. It is a branch of the science of *linguistics*, the scientific study of languages. It should be emphasized that we have a rather special problem in carrying out any sort of analysis of language and meaning, because the analysis itself has to be described *in a language*. It is easy to become confused between the words we are using to do the describing and the words we are describing. As a result we must know when we are talking about words, and when we are talking about the things that words *stand for*.

In the above paragraph we have used two important semantic devices, apart from ordinary grammar, to try to clarify our meaning. Firstly, the word 'semantics' was put in single quotation marks (' ') so that we know it is *the word* that is meant. We must always remember to distinguish between a word such as 'pencil' and the thing we use to write with.

Secondly we used italics for the words 'stand for' because there is something rather special about these words and we want them carefully noticed. In fact the words 'stand for' above were vague in meaning, and such vagueness when it occurs in an argument needs to be emphasized. This sort of thing is a part of semantic analysis, so we shall now expand these points a little further.

Consider again the sentence 'Bath is in Somerset'. It should be noticed that we use double quotation marks for sentences we are *talking about*, or when we are quoting people's words. Now suppose we said 'Bath has four letters'. It is fairly clear in fact that the two words 'Bath' in the two sentences are in some way different. In the first sentence we are talking about the town itself and using the word to indicate the town, whereas in the second case we are talking about the word itself. We must distinguish carefully between labels and the things (or ideas) labels are attached to.

If I say 'The world is square', you cannot know for certain whether I am mistaken about the empirical facts – do I really regard the world as having a square shape? Or am I misusing the word 'square'? Either could be the case, so we can easily imagine the same sort of confusions occurring in the constructions of science which are verbal models of reality.

It is clear that we must try to maintain the distinction between words and their referents as they are sometimes called.

The word 'pencil', for example, refers to all the *referents* which are pencils. Already one can glimpse the difficulties involved in talking about talking, or for that matter writing about writing.

The next point is about *vagueness*, in words or phrases. We can use italics to draw attention to any important vagueness of word or phrase. We might have guessed from the start that language is always more or less vague, but we accept this as inevitable, and note that what is important is that we, when using language, should recognize (i.e. *be thoroughly aware of*) that vagueness.

Semantics is often concerned with the classification of meaning, but sometimes also the word 'semantics' is used in a narrower sense to describe the association of words with references or labels with objects, and sometimes it is used to describe the broader field of the analysis of meanings in conversation or in writing.

The essential link between language, complex learning, and thinking comes about because, as we have said, we learn *by description*. This has its origins in symbol learning which, we must recall, is a type of conditioning, sometimes called 'instrumental conditioning'.

Thinking almost certainly takes place in language, since we store linguistic information, and we are able to argue logically from the linguistic information we store. The very fact that we are able to associate a name successfully with an object is clear evidence that the name and the thing named are both stored.

We should also add that the future of psychology is almost certain to be built up around the use of language. It is a vital feature of cognition that has been greatly neglected in the past, and we might expect to see this rectified, and fairly soon.

There is at least one quite different approach to language that regards languages as physical things. Language, when spoken, involves a complicated physiological process in the mouth and speech organs of the speaker, as well as complicated physiological processes in the hearer, set up by vibrations of the air. The human ear picks up these vibrations and recodes them into pulses in the nervous system. The brain collects these pulses through the nerves running from the ears and decodes them into the original ideas of the speaker. The fact that the translation (decoding) is often approximate is part of the reason for the very existence of the science of semantics. The uses of language involve physiological, physical, and psychological processes, and we are particularly concerned with the relation between language and thought. But we must also look at the relation of language to sensation and perception.

Speaking involves the use of the larynx, throat, and breathing apparatus, as well as the brain itself. Hearing involves picking up the physical vibrations of the air, first in the outer ear, and then to the middle ear, which transmits the vibrations mechanically to the inner ear, which stimulates the auditory nerve, and this in turn stimulates the auditory sections of the brain. This sort of process was sketched out in Chapter 2.

The visual speech area is in that part of the brain concerned with vision in general, situated at the back of the head.

The auditory speech area is in that part of the brain concerned with hearing; it is at the side of the head. There is little doubt that the ability to see and hear words and sentences has gradually emerged from the capacity to see and hear anything at all. In the same way as seeing and hearing always involve recognition and understanding, so seeing and hearing words involves interpreting or *decoding* what we call the 'meaning' of the words, although meaning is primarily related to sentences rather than words in isolation. The motor speech area is concerned with the actual utterance of the sounds that make up speech. The motor speech area is a rather specialized centre that has emerged in the brain during the course of evolution. It is one of many such motor centres that has a relatively specific controlling function on the body's physical actions.

All that needs to be said at the moment about the purely neurophysiological factors, involving semantics and the brain, is that the brain acts as a storage centre for information and has the ability to *abstract,* to *generalize,* and to *utilize* such *information.* The brain specifically stores information that is fed in through hearing (spoken words) and seeing (written words), and the association centres of the brain are almost certainly responsible for the processes of recognition which are so closely bound up with the 'meaning' of language. This is all very closely connected with the process of learning by description.

Summary

There are a number of principles and conditions that affect human learning. The principle of reinforcement accounts for learning through reward or avoidance of punishment. The three effects of every learning experience are: the communication of knowledge, the development of skills, and the shaping of attitudes. These are accomplished by such conditions as motivation of the student, distribution of practice, and feedback of results. Learning is accomplished more effectively if the material is meaningful to the student. Our learning, overall, is a process of associations. These associations will lead us to transfer our responses to new situations. We learn to think and solve problems by both convergent and divergent thinking.

The most important single feature of complex human learning is language. Languages are made up of symbols and signs, and these must be learned in the same way as other things are learned. Once they have been learned then they and the way the brain associates them directly influence our further learning.

FURTHER READING

Mace, C. A., *The Psychology of Study*, Penguin, 1962

Mowrer, O. H., *Learning Theory and Behaviour*, New York, Wiley, 1960

Mowrer, O. H., *Learning Theory and the Symbolic Process*, New York, Wiley, 1960

Hunt, E. B., *Concept Learning: An Information Processing Problem,* New York and London, Wiley, 1962

CHAPTER SEVEN

MEMORY AND THINKING

HUMAN memory and learning are intimately related since the development of an association between a stimulus and a response requires some sort of a retention process. Some of our associations, such as conditioned reflexes, are not at the conscious, but at the spinal level of association, although possibly they are 'remembered' there also. For most of the behaviour which distinguishes humans from animals (that is thinking and communicating through language) memory is located in the centre of the nervous system on the cortex of the brain. We can think of memory as analogous to some sort of filing cabinet system. Information received through the senses is stored and utilized as needed, within the limits of storage capacity and the personal efficiency for 'searching the files'. (Without this retention process there could be no learned behaviour.) Our storage capacity seems to be an inflexible individual characteristic, but the efficiency with which the information is retrieved is a function of a number of influences. Three of these influences, which are general features in memory, are frequency, recency, and value. *Frequency* refers, everything else being equal, to the tendency to remember those experiences which have happened most often. Experiences or events that occur infrequently are not remembered so well. It is also clear that, everything else being equal, we remember the more recent events in contrast to those that occurred in earlier times. It is as if the old items of information in the 'file' recede towards the back of the 'drawer'. After a long period they tend to be discarded or forgotten. Value refers in general to experiences which are 'more important' or 'more urgent' than others. Each person has his own value system which seems to decide which items are significant and 'placed' where they can be readily 'retrieved'. Other experiences or events which have little importance to the individual are perhaps simply forgotten. Needless to say when older people clearly rewords, including a great number of adjectives. We can use adjectives to qualify objects with such words as 'good', 'clean', 'refined', 'large', and so on. Research has shown that our basic connotive vocabulary can be reduced to the three broad types of adjectives that most people use to describe their environment. The fundamental adjective types are:

> evaluation : i.e. good . . . bad
> potency : i.e. strong . . . weak
> activity : i.e. active . . . passive

These three pairs of adjectives are the basic meanings that we seem to apply to many of the objects we perceive, learn, and think about. The whole field of relationship of symbols and language is the communication process by which human knowledge is recorded and developed. Language makes it possible for each generation to learn for itself what other generations had learned earlier. Knowledge is cumulative, otherwise each generation would have to learn for itself, for example, all of the principles of science. Cognition is the mental process by which we learn, think, and remember; and we use language to describe and understand the world around us.

Summary

Language is the system for representing the objects and ideas that we come to understand and communicate. Language is a complicated process of symbols, signs, and ideas which represents and describes reality as it is, but also according to our own personal understanding of it.

FURTHER READING

Bruner, J. S., Goodnow, J. J., and Austin, G. A., *A Study of Thinking*, New York and London, Wiley, 1956

Bartlett, F. C., *Remembering*, Cambridge University Press, 1932

Bartlett, F. C., *Thinking*, Allen and Unwin, 1958

Hunter, I. M. L., *Memory: Facts and Fallacies* (2nd edition), Penguin, 1964

Thomson, R., *The Psychology of Thinking*, Penguin, 1959

CHAPTER EIGHT

GROWTH AND DEVELOPMENT

THE process of growth and development is something that is taken for granted, since it happens to us all and seems to be a normal, natural series of stages with little variation. Freud focused his attention on the importance of early experience and its long-lasting effects, especially in people with behaviour disorders. One of the important variables which shape our future conduct is the accumulation of experiences that are obtained in the home. In Western society this dependency upon others for satisfaction of basic social and personal needs can last as long as a quarter or a third of a person's lifetime. This is a long time when contrasted with the growth and development rate of other animals. During these formative years we are told when to go to bed, when to rise, what to eat and how, what to wear, how and when to communicate to others, and so on. In comparison with the strong influence of home and family, institutions such as day schools, Sunday schools, and the churches usually have a much smaller effect upon the behaviour patterns of the child.

The two main influences which affect our development are inherited potential and environmental experience. Our inborn characteristics determine our constitution as members of the human species: they determine skin colour, eye colour, bone structure, and internal make-up. These inborn traits govern in a real sense the rate of growth and the limits of biological and physical development.

Some extremists have contended that heredity is the more important determinant of behaviour, implying a mechanistic view of human nature. Others have taken the opposite viewpoint that 'all men are created equal' and the effects of environmental pressures and opportunities cause the main distinction between one man and another. Environment, through learning and experience, certainly nurtures inherited potential so that normal, healthy growth progresses to maturity. The kind of adults we become, however, is the result of the *combined* and *cumulative* effects of these two influences.

To discover the ages and stages of growth, many children have been carefully studied and their behaviour recorded. The early years are essentially concerned with movement and physical development. Mental development also occurs, and this will be discussed later.

From the moment of birth, the child appears as a feeding, crying, sleeping body-waste producer, not very different from any other infant creature. None of the human characteristics, such as speech, thought, sociability, and so on, are apparent. Within a few weeks the child's muscles mature enough for him to be able to focus his eyes on things and people around him, and show an awareness of his environment. The reflex patterns of behaviour that are inborn include sucking, breathing, and the other body functions. The infant is so helpless that he cannot even perform such basic survival responses as escape from pain-causing stimuli, or obtaining food and drink, without adult assistance. By six months he can sit up, and at the end of the first year he is usually able to stand or crawl around. Within two or three months more he is on his feet and walking without assistance. Speech development takes place in a somewhat similar manner. In the early months the only sounds are crying or babbling noises. After six months, distinct learned speech sounds can be made, such as 'mamama' and 'dadada'. By the first year these have become 'Mama' and 'Daddy', and are associated with particular people. Although the spoken vocabulary is quite limited at this age, quite a few commands and demands can be clearly understood by the child, such as 'sit still' or 'open wide', or 'don't touch that'. By about fifteen months the child is able to issue one-word demands or comments such as 'out' or 'doll'. Soon, the words are connected in crude but meaningful combinations of two or three words: 'me want sweet' and 'me play toys'. The child is now becoming a human being, to be influenced by the experiences which make people social.

Research with animals and humans has shown, however, that our psychological needs and motives may be significantly influenced from the day of birth, if not before. The importance of the sense of touch and other forms of early behaviour experience has been highlighted by studies of monkeys brought up in isolation with only a choice of substitute mothers to comfort them. One of the 'mothers' was a roughly monkey-shaped construction of wire, with an indentation in its 'chest' where a milk-filled bottle could be sucked so that nourishment could be obtained in the normal way. The other 'mother' was a frame of wire, covered in sponge and wrapped in towelling material. This one was for some of the animals also provided with a source of nourishment. Nearly all the monkeys, regardless of which 'mother' had the bottle, spent virtually all of their time in the presence of the soft, cuddly substitute mother. Not only was she a comfortable thing to cling to but, when the young animals were frightened, they returned to her as the source of protection and safety. The experience and association with the cuddly substitute mother was long-lasting, and when a monkey was returned to her after a full year of separation he demonstrated a very real affection and pleasure at the reunion. (See plate 3a.)

These experiments, reported by Dr Harry Harlow of Wisconsin University, were originally intended to test the relative strengths of the oral and sucking need against the need for contact-comfort. The studies demonstrated the greater importance of the sense of touch in these animals, but they also brought out some very startling side effects.

When the monkeys, brought up in isolation, were put in cages with others of the opposite sex, with the intention of breeding from them, it was found that they were all very anti-social! Not only would they not associate with each other, but those few who tried to engage in the sex act were just not able to assume a correct posture. Most of the monkeys were without any sex drive, instinct or the 'savoir faire' necessary for reproduction! This was most disturbing. If the monkeys would not breed, an enormous cost would have to be born to continue the experiments.

Dr Harlow set a couple of normal male monkeys to engage some of the reluctant females in sexual activities. As a result of the skill and patience of these 'Romeos' some of the females became pregnant. When they gave birth to their offspring, however, they treated them as unwanted children, or abandoned them altogether. These females appeared to be without maternal drive or mothering instinct.

Although, of course, it would be wrong to draw firm conclusions about human behaviour on the basis of these studies of monkeys, Dr Harlow's experiments strongly suggest that contact-comfort may be very important to a child. They also suggest that isolation during very early childhood can lead to: (a) antisocial behaviour as an adult, (b) absence of interest or ability to engage in sexual affairs, and (c) among the females, a lack of maternal drive. These motivational consequences were completely unexpected and are now being intensively studied in an effort to throw more light upon types of childhood experiences and their relationship with motivation in later life. Orphanages, where similar results of behaviour disturbance were once observed, today try to make provision for every child to receive, as a protective measure, a daily 'dose' of love and affection from some adult.

The first five years of human life, spent mostly at home, are characterized by development of language, motor ability, and socialization. The child, however, is quite self-centred in his view of life and generally does not now how to cooperate with other children in play or other activities. Children at this age may play in the same location but there is no genuine understanding one for the other. School experiences, however, open up a whole new world for the child. He learns to become partly independent of his mother and his home. He learns new facts of life, such as the distinction between the sexes, emphasized by the different toilet arrangements. He learns to conform to a greater extent than might have been the case at home. School uniforms, communal meals, scheduled play and rest periods, all are part of the school experiences of learning how to behave in society.

As the child matures he develops more complex powers of reasoning. With exposure to stimulating material in the school environment the child rapidly acquires many intellectual skills, including the ability to use symbols such as letters and numbers. This acquisition of knowledge is also integrated with the development of other skills, such as the ability to play certain games, the use of artistic materials, tools, etc., and the formation of attitudes. The schools are charged with the task of inculcating knowledge and also moulding the children into useful members of their community and society. To achieve these multiple objectives the schools include recreational activities as well as lessons in academic subjects, so that mental and physical development are stimulated at the same time.

During adolescence the child undergoes changes in his psychological make-up as important and significant as those in the first five years of life. During this period between the dependency of childhood and the freedom of adulthood, the physical, social, and emotional changes that occur sometimes cause dramatic open conflict between the adolescent, his parents, and society. This, of course, is not true of all teenagers, and many youngsters ripen into adulthood with little or no difficulty.

As the adolescent becomes older and stronger and gains more freedom, he may abuse his independence or he may become shy and withdrawn. Many adjustments have to be made, many skills learned, and many new styles of behaviour have to become a part of the normal life of the individual. Height and weight increase very rapidly, the sex organs mature, and the child is now biologically able to be a parent. Boys find that they need to shave and girls round out into noticeable womanhood. Generally, girls enter adolescence two years earlier than boys, and between the ages of eleven and fifteen many girls are taller than boys. Age eleven is the typical beginning of the adolescent stage for girls and age thirteen for boys. During adolescence the rate of growth is faster than at any other stage since early infancy.

Adolescence is frequently described as 'the awkward age', but in point of fact there is generally no loss in physical skill or coordination. Tests of physical skills, muscular coordination, and athletic ability show a steady increase in ability during the transitional years. Why then do adolescents appear to be so uncoordinated and incompetent? Perhaps it is because we expect them to behave like the seventeen- or eighteen-year-olds that they in part resemble, rather than the twelve- to sixteen-year-olds that they are. Adjustment expresses itself in various forms. The more noticeable problems are insufficient skill and knowledge in making the appropriate responses to different situations. In the past, parents, teachers, and other adults were in a position of greater authority than today; now the greater freedom and independence allowed to the adolescent by society increases his uncertainties. How does one ask a girl out to a dance? When should one plan to meet her family? A girl living alone or sharing a flat produces a situation that can be awkward for both boy and girl. These are very real problems to the adolescents and they will make mistakes in the process of growing up and learning. In full-time employment, an entirely new experience, the teenager has to learn a novel set of approved manners and behaviour. This uncertainty about what to do is reflected often in inconsistent work and expressions of great fatigue. Part of the time there may be intensive concentration and effort to get on with the job, but at other times the young worker may relax into childish pranks and irrational activities. Smoking, the wearing of adult clothing and cosmetics, vigorous debate about practical and theoretical issues, all are part of the process of development into adulthood. Some may make exaggerated efforts to pass as adults, while others may cling to their lost childhood and dependence. Interest in the opposite sex and the desire to avoid conflicts and problems result in a new set of difficulties. The sex problem in Western civilization is created in part by the conflict between physical readiness for adult sexual behaviour and the cultural prohibition of intercourse before marriage. Other cultures may have formal initiation ceremonies in which the child is publicly and formally inducted into the adult society. The ceremonies may be painful but the transition period is short, and little of our modern uncertainty about behaviour is found in those cultures.

If a single word were needed to characterize adolescence it would be 'freedom'. The problems of this age are quite similar to the problems faced by new nations or former colonies which are obtaining independence. They want to be treated like adults and also wish the parent to have tolerance for their efforts to be individualistic, regardless of the consequences. The transition is made most smoothly if the change is anticipated and provisions are made through which the child naturally assumes more and more independence.

To help themselves over the uncertainties and the feelings of insecurity that permeate this stage of life, teenagers have found that grouping together is an aid to self-protection and psychological self-preservation. There is strength and sympathy and comradeship among members with the same problems.

These groupings, formal or informal, may result in common mannerisms, like choosing to wear the same type of dress, having the same style of haircut, participating in the same activities, admiring the same pop idols. Fortunately, almost all adolescents, in every generation, overcome their difficulties, aided by effort and understanding on the part of their parents (all former adolescents!) and grow up to be normal adult members of the community.

Summary

Childhood development is the result of the combined influence of learning and inborn determinants of growth. Early experiences and the giving or withholding of love can have important consequences upon the child's normal growth. Adolescence is characterized by significant bodily changes, the attainment of sexual maturity, and many changes of attitude, outlook, and social behaviour.

FURTHER READING

Hurlock, E. B., *Adolescent Development* (3rd edition), New York and London, McGraw-Hill, 1966

Jersild, A. T., *The Psychology of Adolescence*, Macmillan, New York, 1957

CHAPTER NINE

INTELLIGENCE AND ABILITY TESTING

WHEN we talk of *intelligence*, we usually think in terms of the ability to solve problems, the ability to learn, mental quickness, imagination, judgement, attention, reasoning, and so on. All of these traits and more may enter into the description of intelligent behaviour. Intelligence is, however, one of the most difficult concepts to define, and many psychologists disagree about a precise definition. One form of operational definition defines intelligence as that which is measured by intelligence tests.

An attempt was made in earlier times to measure intelligence by weighing and dissecting the brain, but these efforts turned out to be fruitless. No conclusive results were found as the brains of genius and idiot were found to be essentially the same in size, weight, and make-up.

Other researchers tried to learn about intelligence by studying the senses and their reactions. They reasoned logically that whatever the mind acquired was obtained through the senses, mainly of vision and hearing. From this they concluded that the individuals who had more highly developed senses – better hearing, keener vision, and faster reaction times – would be the faster and better learners and, consequently, more intelligent people. This attempt to relate speed and sharpness of reaction to school success (the result of mental ability) turned out to be another fruitless effort. The brighter students and the dull ones were found, in balance, to be the same in their sensory abilities.

The first practical approach to the measurement of intelligence, made in 1905, is credited to Dr Alfred Binet. Appointed to study and try to classify bright and dull children in the Paris school system, he decided to collect samples of behaviour in a systematic fashion. These samples were not just any behaviour that could be observed but measureable evidence that could be reported with precision. Dr Binet, working with Dr Simon and other researchers, produced a series of tests and problems derived from the normal daily activities or experiences of the child. These experiences appeared to be typical of the abilities required in the mental functioning, attention, imagination, judgement, and reasoning of children at a particular age-level. Binet assumed that a dull child was like a normal child, only late in his mental development and growth. Various tasks and problems were developed for each age-level. If sixty to ninety per cent of an age group could successfully complete a task, it was considered fair for that age group. If, for example, all eight-year-old children could pass one test, that test was too easy. If nearly all failed, it was too difficult. Only if *most* could pass the test was it considered acceptable for the eight-year-olds. This process was followed for all age groups. Here are some items from the early

TABLE I *Binet Tests for each Age-level*

Age

3 Points to nose, eyes, mouth. Gives family name. Repeats two digits.

4 Gives own sex. Names key, knife, penny. Repeats three digits.

5 Copies a square. Counts four pennies. Unites the halves of a divided rectangle.

6 Counts thirteen pennies. Distinguishes morning from afternoon. Copies a diamond-shape.

7 Shows right hand and left ear. Names four primary colours. Describes a picture.

8 Counts backwards from twenty to zero. Notes omissions from pictures. Gives day and date. Repeats five digits.

9 Recognizes all coins. Names the months of the year in order. Defines familiar words.

10 Criticizes absurd statements. Uses three given words in two sentences or less.

12 Composes one sentence using three given words. Discovers the sense of disarranged sentence.

15 Repeats seven digits. Interprets pictures. Interprets given facts.

Adult gives differences between pairs of abstract terms. Rearranges a triangle in imagination. Gives three differences between a president and a king.

Binet test, showing the various tasks that a French child was expected to do at various ages. Each child tested was given a mental-age score which represented his achievement on this mental test scale.

Now these tests were a very practical approach to the measurement of intelligent behaviour and turned out to be very successful. If a child was found by this method to have a mental age below his calendar age he was identified as retarded. If he was above the mental age of his chronological age-mates, he was considered bright. This brightness can be expressed as a ratio of mental age to calendar age, and we need only multiply it by 100 to make it the intelligence quotient or IQ. The formula is:

$$\frac{\text{mental test age}}{\text{calendar age}} \times 100 = \text{IQ}.$$

For example, take child A, age 10, and child B of the same age. On the mental test, child A gets a mental age of 12, child B, 8. What are their IQs?

for child A: $\dfrac{12}{10} \times 100 = 120$

A has an IQ of 120:
he is bright.

for child B: $\dfrac{8}{10} \times 100 = 80$

B has an IQ of 80:
he is not very bright.

The population average for intelligence is 100, and about half of the general population falls within ten points each side of this middle index score. (Because of certain technical and statistical considerations the IQ is obtained in a slightly more refined fashion than we have indicated here, but this is in essence the method.)

Does this score really represent intelligence? Could not the child being tested have become bored with the test and stopped trying? What if the examiner was a threatening or unpleasant person? The child could have become disturbed by this state of affairs and become unwilling or unable to try to respond with correct answers. What if the child just was not feeling well on the day of the test?

In order to provide a reliable measure of human ability, observations should be (1) neutral and (2) standardized. If the tester was thought to be unfair then another psychologist should administer the test. If the child was not feeling well then we must wait until he has recovered. If the child persists in not making his maximum effort to succeed, then this procedure is not the best one for measuring his intelligence. In virtually all cases of testing mental ability these problems are recognized and adjustments are made.

It should not, of course, be concluded from this that we really *know* what a person's mental abilities are. The test score is an estimate which is precise, standardized, and based upon observable evidence, but it is only an estimate. Until methods and tools are developed for making a more direct measurement of intellectual potential, we can only infer intelligence from the way it shows itself in behaviour. From our observations of what a man does we can conclude what he is. There is substantial evidence which shows these inferences to be reasonably accurate, although there are always some errors in measurement.

In what ways do we try to reduce the errors? First by making our tests as *reliable* as possible. The test score must be a consistent index of ability no matter where or when the person was tested. Without high consistency there can obviously be no precision. Reliability is not enough, however. Psychological tests must also have *validity*. Validity refers to the relationship of test scores to some other external standard of behaviour. A test is valid if it measures what it is intended to measure. For an IQ test to be valid the scores must be highly related to some standard of intelligent behaviour, such as learning performance. Binet's tests were found to be both reliable and valid. The typical child was found to have the same intelligence score when tested a second time. In addition, children judged to be bright, dull, or average by their teachers were in most cases similarly classified by the tests. This reflected the overall validity of the test. (The teachers were not given the test scores before they made their judgements as that would bias the research.) The Binet test, like most tests in use today, was a resounding success for the job it was designed to do. Subsequent to this, mental tests have been developed and used in many countries, but it is in America where they have gained the most favour, and a great deal of test construction and publication takes place in the U.S.A.

In Table 2 we can see how intelligence relates to ability to do things in daily life. This can be interpreted as evidence of the validity of mental tests, but in doing so some caution must be used, as many people hold jobs below their maximum level of abilities. Also, there is a generous overlap between occupational groups.

TABLE 2 *The Relationship of Intelligence to Ability for Certain Jobs*

IQ	Job Capabilities
130	can achieve post-graduate university degrees. Usually fills professional, administrative, or executive jobs.
120	can graduate from university. Fills highly skilled jobs.
110	can complete secondary school and hold skilled jobs.
100	average or typical level. Tend to hold semi-skilled jobs.
90	people here can perform jobs requiring some judgement, such as operating a sewing machine or assembling parts.
75	people at this level can keep a small store, play a musical instrument, or complete primary school.
60	adults at this level are capable of repairing furniture, harvesting vegetables, or assisting an electrician.
50	people here can do simple carpentry or domestic work.
40	dull people here can learn to mow lawns or do simple laundry.

(Taken from Table 20, p. 174 of L. J. Cronbach, *Essentials of Psychological Testing*, 1960.)

Some readers may still object to the whole idea of mental and ability tests on the grounds that they are not perfect measuring devices, and therefore subject to error. This is all very true, but they are the most precise instruments available for measuring such characteristics as mental ability, and they have generally been found to do a better job in assessing intelligence than the judgements of mental ability made by school teachers, personnel officers, and others using interviews only.

What are the components of mental ability? On the basis of many studies we can conceptualize intelligence as a general trait that can be analagous to a pitcher or container. With the growth in years from birth to about eighteen or so it expands in its capacity. How much it contains, of course, depends upon exposure to different learning experiences and information which has been poured into it. From a distant view the container looks as if it has a single compartment, but from close up we can notice different compartments. These sections are the several different traits which make up mental ability overall, and can be described by the tests that measure them. These are tests of verbal comprehension, number manipulation, general reasoning, the ability to see relationships, and other similar characteristics. The process of psychological testing is one of sampling the contents, so to speak. If the test is reliable and valid, the sample will be highly related to the behaviour it is designed to assess and predict. Each of us has a mental potential, determined by inheritance, but the extent to which 'the pitcher grows and gets filled up', is determined by our environment and education.

Psychological tests may be used for evaluating characteristics other than intelligence. A test may be used to predict future performance in mathematics classes. In this kind of application the test is intended to measure *aptitude* which is *the ability to profit from future training*. Another test may also be used at the end of the mathematics course to measure how much the student has learned. This test is an achievement test. An *achievement* test is designed to measure *amount of learning from past training and experience*.

There are many different kinds of aptitude and achievement tests. They vary from mechanical aptitude and musical ability tests to measures of language aptitude and social relations achievement. There are tests for measuring ability to be a radio operator or a pilot. Readers who are interested in being tested on their vocational abilities should contact the local schools career teacher or their local employment officer who can refer them to the appropriate agency.

TABLE 3 *Test Scores and Flight Training Results*

Score Level	Successes (%)	Failures %
9	96	4
8	91	9
7	86	14
6	79	21
5	71	29
4	61	39
3	48	52
2	34	66
1	24	76

In order to make clear the usefulness and the limitations of ability tests, here is one illustration. During the Second World War over 160,000 trainees for pilot training were tested by the U.S. Air Force. Their scores were translated into overall marks on a scale from 9 down to 1. Among those who got full marks, only four in one hundred failed the flight training programme. On the other hand, three quarters of those with lowest marks could not graduate from training, or crashed their planes during training. The tests were not perfect, but they performed a very useful service, saving lives as well as time and money, by assuring that only the men with the highest potential for graduation were accepted for training.

There are many intelligence tests which have been published since Binet's in 1905. Some of them are designed to be given to one person at a time, others are group tests, still others are non-verbal tests and performance tests. The testing movement has come a long way in this half-century but there are still many improvements to be made. Tests must be made as reliable as possible, and they must also be as valid as possible if they are to do the job for which they are designed.

Summary

Intelligence tests that are reliable, valid, and standardized are successful tools for measuring mental ability. The IQ is an expression of the ratio of intelligence to calendar age. Mental ability comprises verbal comprehension, number skills, reasoning, space visualization, and other problem-solving traits. Aptitude tests assess learning potential; achievement tests assess the success of learning experiences.

FURTHER READING

Cronbach, L. J., *Essentials of Psychological Testing* (2nd edition), Hamish Hamilton, 1960
Tyler, L. E., *Tests and Measurements*, New Jersey and London, Prentice-Hall, 1963

CHAPTER TEN

ATTITUDES AND PUBLIC OPINION

HUMAN behaviour may be understood in part merely by observing people reacting to their environment. Behaviour is often a subtle, shaded kind of action, and when it is manifested by answers to direct questions we find that these answers are given in extremes, in terms of black or white, yes or no, all or none; only seldom in relative terms. The citizens of other countries are either 'good' or 'bad'. The way in which we look at our environment is a reflection of our general attitude.

The tendency to regard things with approval or disapproval is called an *attitude*. A more precise definition is: *the feeling towards or against an object*. Attitude objects may be people, places, things, or even ideas! The kinds of attitudes that a person displays may be established and seen as a picture of his unique feelings towards his world. One man may be favourably inclined towards a Tory government, low personal taxes, and free competition in business. We would note such a man as a conservative. But another man may also support the Conserva-

1 A 'distorted' room

2 The visual cliff

3a The chimpanzee claims his reward

3b An infant rhesus monkey with two artificial mothers

4a The Bristol Tutor

4b The Bristol Tutor Room at Plymouth College of Technology

tive Party in political affairs, yet be more favourably inclined towards greater government control of business and the economy. He too would be called conservative, but to a less degree (a moderate conservative?). Although we label each man with the same tag they differ sharply over policies within the category of conservatism. One may support a plan for Great Britain to affiliate with other European nations; the second man may denounce this idea.

The constellation of attitudes that each of us has towards people, places, ideas, and things marks the uniqueness of the individual as much as height, weight, facial features, etc. We learn to recognize people by their external characteristics, but also by their internal characteristics (attitudes). Yet in spite of the obvious differences between people, there is, perhaps surprisingly, great similarity in attitudes, and psychologists are able to identify, and predict, clusters of similarities forming persistent attitudes. From these measurements some understanding of human behaviour can be obtained and some predictions can be made about future conduct and action.

Stereotypes are examples of attitudes of certain kinds with respect to peoples of different countries. Europeans tend to think that Americans have horn-rimmed spectacles, hats on the backs of their heads, expensive cameras, and loud voices. The stereotype of the Englishman is of the rather pompous, military-looking man with bowler hat and umbrella. These stereotypes are of course, at best, caricatures of certain small minority groups which become generalized to a whole nation. The dangers inherent in these attitude-generalizations are sufficiently obvious.

As intelligence is estimated by obtaining samples of intelligent behaviour, so attitudes are obtained by assessing opinions. Personal opinion is the visible top of an iceberg of invisible attitudes. The measurements are carried out by interviews, questionnaires, polls, and controlled observation of behaviour, where matters of fact and opinion are usually correlated. Here are some examples of opinion measurement questions:

Single Question

What brand of soap powder is used in your household? If there was a General Election tomorrow, which party would you vote for? Do you favour a change in the number of television channels? If so, what change? On which channel did you watch the Queen's Christmas Day speech?

The single question elicits a straightforward, simple opinion-response. If people of similar incomes, or class, or occupation are pre-chosen for quizzing, the answers could reflect accurate estimates of their group behaviour. Public-opinion poll-takers, by following certain procedures in selecting their samples, have attained results which are subsequently accurate for 98–99 per cent of the voters. The few people who are undecided in the surveys frequently fall half and half into each category, and generally these respondents do not interfere with the total prediction.

To obtain results with only a small margin of error, a great deal of effort goes into the preparation of questions, the recording of answers, and the statistical treatment of the data. First, the questionnaire is clearly worded to prevent ambiguity or misunderstanding. Also, the questions must not restrict the respondent in such a way that all possible answers are inadequate to express his views. In the political polls, the respondent is not asked: 'Do you plan to vote for the Conservative candidate in the next election?' This approach begs for an affirmative reply, since it seems that the surveyor is trying to determine the amount of Conservative support he can muster. If sincere and accurate replies are desired, then the question must leave the respondent free to choose from any reasonable alternative.

Because of the critical importance of the wording of the question, preliminary studies are conducted to assess the value of the questions in advance. In this way, ambiguity, vagueness, and accidental bias can be avoided. These problems can be categorized as:

1. bias in the question,
2. bias in the sponsorship, and
3. bias of the interviewer.

Sampling

The opinion-surveyor faces other problems. How can he obtain a sample of opinions without going out and surveying the entire population? How can he obtain a *sample* of people who are truly representative of the population? One approach is to take an alphabetical list of the entire population and to draw out every thousandth name. This gives a reasonable assurance of a proper sampling of age groups, economic classes, minority groups, etc. Another way is to take a county which has been demonstrated in the recent past to be representative and to poll the people who live in the different areas. The choice of the areas polled is very much like drawing names out of a hat. The area is divided into equal squares and each is numbered; then the numbers actually *are* drawn out of a hat. Each area has an equal chance to be drawn, and if a sufficient number of areas are selected, the people in them will be found to be a useful sample of the entire area. The descriptive characteristics of the sample are compared with information from the census to make sure that the chosen few are truly representative of the whole area.

Political pollsters find this procedure to be an expensive one, and frequently compromise by establishing a quota system. A quota system fixes the numbers of respondents to be surveyed on the basis of census information. (If the population is fifty per cent male then half of the people polled will be of that sex.) The quotas usually indicate the sex, age, income, and residence of the respondent. Using proper scientific controls, one may produce a reliable survey with a minimum of expense and effort. (The slight loss in precision of this method is partly a function of the responses obtained. In an election poll, when the voters are evenly divided, however, any error can lead to a wrong prediction. If the respondents are, on the other hand, strongly in favour of only one side of a question, a few percentage points in either direction will be unimportant.) The final number in the sample can be a relatively small one, and a few thousand people can in theory be quite representative of, say, the population of the British Isles.

Panels

Organizations such as advertising agencies are interested in a continuous measurement of attitude towards the products which they promote. They find that their needs can frequently be satisfied by surveying groups of half a dozen people at a time, or about one hundred altogether. These groups, often composed of housewives, meet for two hours or so and look at various advertisements of the agency and at those of its competitors. They may also examine products and report their experiences with them. All this is intended to reveal the inclinations of people towards the attitude-objects. Statements by those who use the product and by those who avoid it are assessed, for copy ideas may rise from both 'pro' and 'con' attitudes. More effective ways of selling the product may even be suggested by someone who resents current materials. This small sample or panel procedure is used with great caution, as the members tend to develop 'panelitis', a disease of becoming an 'expert' in advertising methods. When members begin to show the symptoms of reporting what people should do and feel, rather than what they do and feel, then they are dropped from the panel. Panels usually rotate their members about once a year.

Questionnaire Methods

Whatever type of sample chosen, and method employed to obtain it, the next major problem is to choose a questionnaire form which will elicit genuine opinions. If interviewers are to be used to gather the data they must be rigorously trained. Training assures understanding of the questionnaire, so interviewers will be set to perceive a respondent's relevant comments. Also, the trained interviewer will be less likely to bias the data by interjecting into the interview his own personal opinions about the things being surveyed.

The classical method of attitude scaling is 'equal appearing intervals'. A list is composed of statements about the object to be surveyed. These statements are judged by a sample of people on their *degree* of favourableness. After statistical treatment, these judgements are arranged into a scale somewhat like the following (this scale is intended to measure attitudes towards television. The respondent checks the statement or statements which most clearly represent his *feelings* about television):

☐ Television appeals to man's highest nature.
☐ Television is increasing its value to society.
☐ Television is not sufficiently appreciated by the general public.
☐ Television does more good than harm.
☐ The good and bad points of television balance each other.
☐ Television is decreasing in its value to society.
☐ The past of television is disgraceful.
☐ Television appeals to man's lowest nature.
☐ Television is an enemy of truth.

Point values for each statement are pre-determined, and the best items are arranged (as above) in decreasing order of favourability. The higher on this scale that your feelings are rated, the more favourable is your attitude towards television.

This method is relatively easy to administer and score, but the results obtained are limited in use. The average degree of favourableness to television may be obtained, and the amount by which people vary in their intensity may be obtained, but *why* they have their particular opinion remains unexplored.

A more resourceful way to get this same kind of information, and also the reasons for these opinions, is 'summated ratings'. This consists of a series of multiple-choice items which explore different aspects of the central attitude object.

Mark the answer which best expresses your feelings.
1. Television is an important source of communication.
    ☐ strongly agree
    ☐ tend to agree
    ☐ tend to disagree
    ☐ strongly disagree
2. Adult education programmes should be offered more frequently on television.
    ☐ strongly agree
    ☐ tend to agree
    ☐ tend to disagree
    ☐ strongly disagree

Each item is scored as favourable or unfavourable towards television, and a total score of attitude is obtained this way. In addition, specific opinions on many aspects of television are obtained. Whatever the overall opinion, explicit information is also available about what contributed to that overall attitude. This questionnaire form can be expanded even further. If a line of space is provided between each item for remarks by the respondent, then spontaneous comments are brought in which can be as informative as the whole questionnaire.

The main disadvantage of this method is that quite a bit of effort and statistical analysis is required before a reliable questionnaire can be constructed.

A more indirect method of opinion measurement, called the error-choice or direction of perception technique, may be used where the sponsor does not wish to reveal the objective of his research. This questionnaire arrangement appears to be an information test, which in part it is. Half the items are straightforward information or knowledge test items, but the remaining items are attitude items which *appear* to be information items. Either the attitude items are constructed with statements which have no known answer, or the answer is not provided. The direction of error in the response chosen indicates the attitude that is held by the respondent. Of the two questions below, the first is an information test question, and the second is an attitude item.

1. The number of television channels controlled by the Independent Television Authority (I.T.V.) is:
   (a) none   (b) one   (c) two   (d) three

2. The proportion of viewers who watched I.T.V. regularly in 1962 was about:

   (a) 25%   (b) 35%   (c) 75%   (d) 85%

The correct answer to the second question is about fifty per cent, and the direction of response chosen would tend to indicate attitudes towards I.T.V. A large assortment of these types of items would supply an estimate of both knowledge about television and also opinions about television. One of the problems that immediately occurs to the psychologist asked to construct a questionnaire of this type is the ethical one. Most psychologists refuse to use this instrument because it masks its true purpose and such procedures are of questionable propriety. In spite of this, it has been used for measuring the opinions of applicants for employment and employers have gained relevant information through deception. It has also come into use as a subtle device for collecting political opinions. Because of its questionable ethics, and the great expense in constructing the questionnaire, the direction of perception method is seldom employed.

Survey Uses

The attitude survey has been used for a large number of objectives, and it may be remembered that we mentioned this in Chapter 1 as one of the main psychological techniques for the measurement and assessment of *group* characteristics. The most widely known application is in estimating public opinion towards the political parties and the party leaders. This kind of poll receives the most publicity because a newspaper usually sponsors the research. Advertising agencies conduct assessments of public opinion and attitudes on a continuous basis. Large industries also perform periodic surveys of their employees. The objective is usually to assess motivations and morale in the organization. These polls are conducted annually to uncover the general feelings among the workers and staff, and also to assess the effect of any changes in policies and practices which may have occurred since the previous survey. Individual political candidates have been known to make a survey of their 'public image' prior to promoting a campaign. These surveys reveal the issues to which the public are most responsive, and also the kinds of pronouncements that the public would like to hear !

One of the important parts of any attitude survey, the statistical analysis of the results and the testing of inferences and conclusions, is a special, technical aspect of all surveys. The analysis may be a simple count of the frequency of responses for each type of reaction. More often, the data are cross-checked, with a comparison of personal characteristics against the different qualities of opinion. This cross-checking brings out further information about the relationship of responses to the various factors accounting for the particular opinions held. From continuous analysis of such information much human behaviour can be accurately predicted: for example, the results of many years of political opinion polling around the world show that in Western democratic countries, in general, the man who tends to turn out on election day is the man with more education, a higher income, in middle age, and who is male, white, and an established resident in the community. (European workers vote in large numbers, but in America workers tend to abstain.) The attitudes of these people described are typically inclined towards the conservative position on many of the political issues.

The majority of the general public are usually moderate or liberal in opinions, rather than conservative, and yet conservative governments are elected with greater frequency. Why? Because, though conservative supporters are fewer in numbers, *they exercise their vote in greater proportion to their numbers*. The issue of the political parties can be described as one of getting out the vote, which is a prime Labour Party objective. Conservative Party objectives are to publicize the issues and persuade people towards the conservative attitude. The proportion of people who are uncertain in their attitudes about the political parties is large enough in numbers to make most major elections well-matched contests. If attitudes are relatively stable characteristics, why is there so much variation in the governments that may be elected from one time to the next? Mainly because the voters retain their basic attitude orientation, but they view each election in relation to their current general attitude. If they feel strongly concerned about the outcome of an election, then the deep underlying attitude is the main determinant of behaviour. If the contest is regarded as a less personal concern then the individual may not vote at all, or if he does, it may be for the party out of power. Some people who feel that this is rather too far removed from their own views will tend to vote for the Liberal Party.

One final caution in this general topic of attitude. Although group behaviour can be predicted with remarkable accuracy, attitude measurements will not predict reliably how any one *individual* will invariably vote. An individual may be inconsistent and irrational, but paradoxically a population is consistent and predictable.

Summary

An attitude is a feeling towards or against an object. Attitudes are assessed through panel groups, area samples, and other large group-selection methods. Opinions, the expressions of attitudes, are obtained through interviews, use of single questions, 'equal appearing interval' questionnaires, 'summated rating' questionnaires, direction of perception methods, and other techniques. Surveys are used for assessing political opinions, evaluating advertisements, measuring worker morale, and other diverse applications. Although attitudes are not precisely measured, accurate predictions of group behaviour can be made.

FURTHER READING

Cantril, H., *Gauging Public Opinion*, New Jersey, Princeton University Press, 1944
Eysenck, H. J., *The Psychology of Politics*, Routledge and Kegan Paul, 1954

CHAPTER ELEVEN

FRUSTRATION

WE said in an earlier chapter that human behaviour is motivated by needs and drives and that the individual is constantly seeking goals which he hopes will satisfy those needs and drives. There are many occasions, however, when a person is in some way prevented from achieving his goals and as a consequence his motivation is frustrated.

Frustration can occur in a number of different ways. It can occur when some person or object or state of affairs blocks the individual's path to his goal. A man may be deprived of deserved promotion in his job by a superior who has a personal grudge against him. He may miss his favourite television show because the receiver has broken down. His holiday may be spoilt by bad weather. All these are examples of frustration arising from the individual's environment.

Other sources of frustration can be found within the individual himself. His own limitations may prevent him from achieving certain goals. His desire to reduce his golf handicap may be frustrated by his lack of skill at the game. His ambition to be successful in business may be frustrated by insufficient intelligence, knowledge, or hard work.

Another very potent source of frustration is motivational conflict. The individual fails to satisfy a need because he is unable to choose between two or more courses of action which are open to him.

One kind of conflict occurs when one has to choose between two equally attractive goals such as the desire to save money and the equally strong desire to buy new clothes. If these are of the same intensity and if achieving the one means giving up the other we are upset with the difficulty of the choice. We may vacillate and be unable to act.

Another type of conflict occurs in the presence of two equally repellent threats, when again we are caught in between. One may be afraid to ask one's employer for an increase in salary, but also be equally afraid to go home and face the wrath of one's wife for not doing so. This state of affairs also makes life difficult.

A third type of conflict situation consists in the pursuit of a goal which represents both a threat and an attraction at the same time. When thinking of applying for a new job we may be attracted by the better opportunities that the prospective employer offers, but we may also be repelled by the threat of being tested and interviewed, and perhaps being rejected after all.

When we meet one of these problems and fail to resolve it

successfully we develop a feeling of disturbance and discomfort. In an attempt to relieve this feeling we may react in various different ways.

One way of trying to overcome an obstacle is by striking out against it. This outward expression is called aggression. How many times have we kicked at some inanimate object because it was in the way or causing us annoyance? Aggression is most often displayed by children when they are frustrated. They strike out at their toys, parents, sisters or brothers, or whatever else they perceive to be thwarting them. If you hammer your thumb instead of a nail you will probably throw the hammer down as if to punish it for the error of its ways. Aggression, however, is not always expressed so directly. You may carefully place the hammer down and then vent your aggressive feelings on your wife or some other innocent bystander. Aggression is often displaced against other people or objects, as if they were the cause of the trouble. Mental health and adjustment is largely a matter of the style of behaviour employed to express one's feelings of aggression. The gardener who, in response to frustration, attacks the weeds in his garden is acting in a constructive, socially approved way. If, however, he beats his children or attacks other people, then society will impose restrictions upon his freedom of action.

Not all people behave aggressively when they are frustrated. Some may become apathetic and inattentive and withdraw from the situation. The world of imagination is a comforting retreat from reality: it can be made as accommodating as we choose.

A different pattern of behaviour which often follows frustration is to act in a stereotyped, persistent manner. The same behaviour is blindly, unsuccessfully repeated over and over again, although it is not solving the problem. A man will go through all his pockets six or seven times in search of a missing theatre ticket although it is quite evident at once that he has left it at home. Despite this he persists, unable to break the chain that ties him to his behaviour. We like to believe we are always rational and under complete control of our actions, but this is obviously far from true.

These habitual, common reactions to frustration are called

defence mechanisms. They are called 'mechanisms' because they are unconscious processes. The individual is not aware of their operation and does not deliberately employ them. They protect the individual self-image and relieve the disabling effects of excessive tension and frustration. They both maintain and even increase self-esteem. They are particularly useful in cases of frustration caused by personal limitations and failings.

The common defence mechanisms are rationalization, projection, identification, reaction-formation, repression, and substitution. We will define and illustrate each one in turn.

Rationalization is the psychological process of explaining away situations in which we find ourselves in such a way as to justify our actions. If you were late for work today, was it because the car would not start, or the train was late – or was it really because you failed to get up early enough? Frequently heard rationalizations are: 'I do not want central heating because it reduces the fresh air in the home.' The truth is very likely: 'I cannot afford central heating because I do not earn enough.' Such excuses are rationalizations *only* when they operate as self-deceptions. A statement that sounds like an excuse may be a genuine explanation if it coincides with the objective facts. Today you may have lost your way travelling across country and rationalized your frustration by saying that you had a desire to see the countryside. Tomorrow you may deliberately choose the same route in order to see the countryside. In the latter case there is no rationalization and no self-deception. If you get lost, though, you will undoubtedly try hard to think up another excuse or new rationalization!

Projection is the response pattern by which we ascribe to others the undesirable qualities we ourselves have. This defence mechanism, if used in excess, is also a retreat from reality. A man who is disagreeable and unsociable may complain that other people are unfriendly and spiteful. We tend to see in others our own faults magnified.

Identification is another mechanism, like projection, but whereas the latter assigns personal faults to others, in identification we take the good qualities of others as our own and enjoy a vicarious feeling of pride and achievement. Our heroes in fiction or real life become our self-images. We may dress like them, have our hair cut in the same style, or even, in the extreme case, walk and talk like them. Adolescents resort to identification in their effort to assert their independence from their parents.

Reaction-formation is the expression of motives opposite to those we really possess. The vocal members of many 'anti' groups are often counter-reacting against the motives they wish to conceal from themselves. An example is a person who may be outspoken for censorship of television, books, and other communication media. He frequently aspires to be the censor, which would require him to be exposed to the material. This desire to experience and enjoy the risqué material is disguised by the outward expression of antipathy. This is not the total explanation of such behaviour, of course. Such people may also take up a clearly reasoned position as well.

Repression is a type of forgetting which is motivated by the unconscious need to deny the memory of any event, and the person who is repressing the past is not aware of his motives. Our tendency to forget our failures and bad times is an illustration of repression. Some kinds of amnesia, or the loss of memory and identity, are an extreme form of repression.

Substitution or sublimation is the means by which we express our anti-social impulses in an acceptable manner. Our desire to commit aggression will get us into trouble if we express it against the man in the street. If we turn to the boxing ring, rugby or football field, or even to weeding the garden, then we not only keep out of trouble but may actually find material and emotional rewards. A mediocre student may make a special effort to excel at athletics. An unathletic student may overwork. Both show a form of behaviour sometimes called compensation or overcompensation, which leads the individual to excessive effort to increase his self-esteem.

These different defence mechanisms are obviously neither independent nor rooted in unambiguous behaviour. Their explanation derives from the different schools of psychoanalytic theory of behaviour which represent a very subjective approach to psychology. Whatever their limitations, they serve as handy labels to mark out the different actions we engage in when we are frustrated and cannot achieve the original goals that we set out to reach. These defence mechanisms are part of the normal, ordinary behaviour patterns that mentally healthy people resort to, and in no way signify a disturbance in personality. They signify personal difficulty only when they are employed to such an excess that the individual loses touch with reality, is unhappy, and, in limited awareness of his shortcomings, becomes in general an inefficient member of his society.

Summary

Conflict and frustration are part of the normal course of life. The habitual reaction patterns to these situations, include aggression, rationalization, projection, identification, reaction-formation, dissociation, repression, and substitution. These defence mechanisms allow us to maintain our self-esteem.

FURTHER READING

Eysenck, H. J., *Fact and Fiction in Psychology*, Penguin, 1965
O.S.S. Assessment Staff, *Assessment of Men*, New York, Rinehart & Co., 1948

CHAPTER TWELVE

ABNORMAL BEHAVIOUR

SOME of the notions about personality development, structure, and function have been treated in the previous chapters, but the nature of normal and abnormal behaviour was not explored. What is meant by normal? How do we classify deviations from the normal? What methods are employed for treating disturbed behaviour?

First, let us try to make clear that normality is relative. It reflects the physical health of the individual, his past experiences, the requirements of his current situation, the standards of the community, and the expectations of our society. What is normal behaviour in military combat (to kill) is not normal in civilian conflict (to argue). What is acceptable behaviour in the Western world is often bizarre and unacceptable in the East. There are residents in mental hospitals who consider their life of free room, board, ample social activity, occupational distraction, and plentiful recreation as normal, healthy, and desirable compared with the life of responsibilities and stresses.

There are different criteria used when it is necessary to enlist the services and facilities of the mental institution. Many patients are institutionalized merely because they are suffering from the deteriorating effects of ageing. Others suffer from brain disorders brought on by chemical poisons to the body such as excessive alcohol, drugs, or other causes of chronic ailment.

If we look at the question of normality in terms of the behaviour of those who are not residing in institutions, we find that some who are not under special care perhaps should be; some suffer from a variety of behaviour problems which are not in themselves disabling but do interfere with happiness, and personal and community relationships. If we can dispense with this idea of normality and abnormality as such, we can achieve a better understanding of behaviour if we think in terms of variety and quality of thought and action.

The terms that are used today to describe those types of behaviour which require special treatment and guidance are embraced under the general category of *mental illness*. Personality disorders can be seen more clearly if we compare an 'abnormal' person with a healthy one, so let us look at the healthy side first. The mentally healthy person can be characterized by a number of traits. He has a workable concept of reality and a reasonably objective understanding of himself. He is aware of the limitations of his own behaviour and the shortcomings of others. In common with his fellow men, he has his share of conflicts, but he is able to recognize and resolve most of them. However, he may not conform and he may even be regarded by some people as eccentric, yet he understands his differences with Society and is not unduly disturbed by these differences.

In addition, the mentally healthy individual is generally also physically healthy and approaches his work and life energetically.

This characterization of mental health as *objectivity, self-awareness, awareness of conflicts,* and *energy* is an attempt to isolate the key elements of an organized life. We can now see mental disorders as deviations from that organization. Disorganized behaviour is not always clear-cut, but like physical illness can be identified by noticing some of its symptoms. Many people lack, to some degree, the above traits. Behaviour problems, like physical illness, are a matter of both quality and amount. One dental cavity is not disturbing to physical health, but a mouthful of such cavities would be a sign of bad health.

The disorders of mental health are generally classified into two broad categories of *neuroses* and *psychoses*. The neuroses are disturbances in behaviour which reflect habit patterns that cope ineffectively with the normal problems of life. The defence mechanisms that a neurotic uses are too inadequate to solve – and often even to identify – his conflicts. He is disorganized. Signs of disorganization are anxiety, fear, obsessive thoughts, compulsion to repeat behaviour and even to develop hysterical reactions like temporary paralysis. The most frequent neurotic symptoms are general anxiety reactions with fear, tenseness, sweating, and nausea. This general fear reaction is not caused by any physical threat, as the behaviour would then be typical and normal. It is rather a general pattern of behaviour that is elicited by many environmental influences which most people find non-threatening. The origins and treatments for neurotic behaviour will be described further in this chapter.

The psychoses are a group of severe behaviour disorders characterized by disturbances in thought and action. The psychotic may be suffering from organic brain damage due to disease, the effects of excessive alcohol, or other physical malfunctions. The general pattern of behaviour includes disturbed thoughts, or delusions, such as the idea that 'my mind is being controlled by radio waves which are being transmitted by some other person'. Delusions of grandeur, divine identity, false memories, and so on are some of the many unreal ideas that psychotics have. These ideas are persistent and bear little relationship to the facts of life. The psychotic does not just think his delusions – he also acts out his private world. A mentally ill person who believes he is Jesus Christ will behave as such, preaching and acting as he believes the role requires. This particular delusion is a common one, and when a psychiatrist finds two of a kind he may arrange a confrontation – 'Jesus, I would like you to meet Jesus'. One of the two patients may give up his delusion under this stress and assume another role, and ofttimes the person who gives up first is the one who is closer to recovery.

Additional symptoms of psychoses are hallucinations and perceptual disorders, such as the hearing of non-existent voices or seeing imaginary figures. Notice that this differs from illusions (mentioned in Chapter 3, Perception) which are reasonable misinterpretations of stimuli. We may all, at times, act in ways similar to those who have neurotic or psychotic symptoms, but the psychotic is distinguished by the persistence and intensity of his delusions. They bear almost no objective relationship to his environment or to the experiences of the other people in his environment.

The psychoses have been traditionally divided into the categories of organic and functional disorders. The organic disorders, mentioned above, are behavioural manifestations of physical illness. The elderly person who is suffering from senile psychosis has a demonstrable deterioration in brain-cell functioning. The person who has suffered from a severe blow to the head may have the same kind of malfunction in which the cells of the brain no longer perform normal functions.

Functional psychoses are disorders which have apparently no observable structural change of body breakdown, and no definable physical cause. These disorders include the extremes of behaviour such as manic-depression, schizophrenia, and paranoia. The manic-depressive swings from extreme despondency to exaggerated overactive elation, and back again. He may stay at the extremes, or he may move through normality. Obviously, not all depressions are psychotic in origin, as personal tragedy can drive our behaviour to that extreme. A psychotic is often a person who acts the way another would act under reasonable stress, but without reasonable cause.

Schizophrenia is the most common type of psychosis. The symptoms are various but they are recognized by behaviour showing disorder of thought and action and flights from reality. Some schizophrenics (called catatonics) withdraw to such an extreme that they may cease to talk and walk.

Various treatments have been tried to bring psychotics back to objective reality or at least to lessen the intensity and frequency of the symptoms. The most successful therapy today entails the use of chemical medications in the form of tranquillizers and a family of drugs called energizers. These medications seem to have an effect upon the chemical processes in the brain, lending support to the idea that the psychoses may have organic causes. Additional support for this view-point comes from the studies of the rate of admissions of mental patients to hospitalization. The number of psychotics in the population tends to be a very constant percentage of the population, and during periods of extreme stress, such as war, depression, etc., there is virtually no change in the percentage of people who become psychotic. A suggestion that the cause of psychosis may be inherited is supported by the discovery that if one identical twin has a psychosis, the odds are 85 in 100 that his twin will also be mentally ill. In fraternal twins, who are like brother and sister in their inherited similarity, the odds drop to about 15 in 100. For the general Western population, on the other hand, the chances that an individual will require treatment for mental illness (which includes both neuroses and psychoses) are about 5 in 100.

Some of the confusion between neurosis and psychosis can perhaps be clarified if we pause and reconsider the neurotic disturbances. Neuroses are regarded as acquired, ineffective behaviour patterns, and these can be demonstrated by human subjects in the laboratory.

The pairing of reward and punishment to the same signal leads to neurotic behaviour. A neurosis can be induced if one signal is taught as a sign of reward and a second signal as a sign of punishment. These signals are then gradually made similar, causing the individual to perch on the point of uncertainty. Neurotic reactions now follow, and when first taught, can be extinguished according to established standard methods. It seems quite clear that some neurotic behaviour is learned and can be modified by schemes for retraining. The psychoses are more difficult to isolate because a patient may be suffering from the effects of an unidentified physical disorder that leads him into habit patterns similar to neurotic behaviour reactions. The functional psychosis, it would seem, is a combination of both neurotic disorganization and psychotic disturbances brought on by brain chemistry disorders.

Virtually all the methods of treatment for neurosis seem to have some effect in relieving the patient. This fact is surprising since different theories of personality lead to radically different treatments and analyses of causes. What may also be surprising is that many people with neurotic behaviour patterns recover from their disturbances with no treatment at all! Perhaps the common element is that of experiences which teach the individual new behaviour patterns. The therapist functions like a teacher overseeing the development of the learning. Life itself is therapeutic, however, and the continuation of work, recreation, duties, and responsibilities can often provide the psychological support to aid the return to reality and personality organization.

Ineffective behaviour, like mentally healthy conduct, does not necessarily occur only when the appropriate occasion calls it forth. Some individuals have behaviour reactions which persist after the cause disappears. A child who was deprived of the necessary tender love and affection he needed during his early years may have learned to distrust all adults and authority. This early lesson in life may lead him to forms of anti-social and delinquent behaviour which can persist through his adult life. If we wish to reform a socially or psychologically disturbed or ineffective person, we cannot hope to expect success by merely advising him to 'pull himself together'. Nor can we depend upon the threat of strong punishment to deter wrong behaviour. This lesson has not been learned since the days when the state hanged pickpockets. Ironically, many pickpockets committed their offences at the public square while the hangings were in progress! Threat of punishment may inhibit some responses, but signal–response–*reward* is the system that leads to new behaviour. A critical examination of the techniques of behaviour change and reform (which is what the psychotherapeutic methods essentially are) reveals two common elements.

One influence that seems to lead mentally disordered people towards improved behaviour is the very nature of the psychological treatment situation itself. In therapy the psychologist or psychiatrist takes great interest in the welfare of his client. This personal relationship of mutual concern may be just what the client needs to help him back on his feet.

The second aid towards recovery is the opportunity provided for learning new ways to behave. The patient is allowed to take trial-and-error actions during the therapy sessions. The therapist, consciously or not, will intermittently reward or reinforce these actions, and these reinforcements lead to new – and soon strengthened – habits of action. A more successful style of life can thus be developed. Mistakes made during these learning sessions carry minimum punishment. The therapist, playing the roles of teacher, coach, friend, parent-substitute, and ordinary citizen, pursues his objective according to a systematic therapeutic framework. He uses his skill and experience to try to reshape the behaviour of a disturbed patient. Such skill is partly an art and may be found not just in the possession of the professional therapist but also in those friends who influence us most.

We can see these common elements in practice if we examine a few traditional methods used to treat disturbed people.

Psychoanalysis, developed by Sigmund Freud, depends upon the development of a close personal relationship between patient and psychoanalyst. The therapy begins with a physical examination to identify organic causes of the disturbance. Interviewing, testing, and personality assessment may then be performed to try to construct a 'picture' of the person's personality. The Freudian therapist, after collecting data about the patient, will then engage the patient in extended interviews. He will search for information about childhood experiences, feelings about parents, anxieties, guilts, obsessions, etc. The patient will be encouraged to make himself comfortable on the now 'almost traditional' couch and talk at random, to say whatever comes into his head, in whatever form he wants to put it, so that his comments can be elicited in a relaxed atmosphere. This flow of talk is called 'free association'. As information about early experiences pours out, the analyst may or may not interpret what he hears. Some analysts are very directive and assume control and authority over their patients. Others prefer to be 'at arm's length', and if the psychoanalyst feels himself becoming emotionally involved, he may try to reduce the development of excessive interdependence. Whatever the amount of control and emotional involvement, the patient metaphorically acts out his anxieties and possibly obtains a better understanding of his faults and fears. He may receive approval from the analyst and this approval stimulates him into probing deeper into his private world. Sometimes an emotional relationship between client and therapist is established and this relationship becomes the analysis. When the person has recovered or improved sufficiently to terminate the sessions, the painful process of separation must be achieved. The patient and psychoanalyst obtain a 'psychological separation or divorce'. With newly gained acceptance and understanding, the client, at least temporarily, is ready to operate with new behaviour patterns. The effectiveness of this method of treatment depends, like all artistic activities, upon the skill of the artist, and the suggestibility of the client. Certain cases such as homosexuals, psychotics, and others having persistent behaviour patterns seem to be virtually invulnerable to analysis.

Another technique, called 'client-centred' or 'non-directive' therapy, has been developed by Carl Rogers. The therapist appears as an intimate, sympathetic friend who wants to help the patient to solve his problems. The initial interview is devoted to explanation of the ground rules that require the client (a) to choose the problems, (b) decide how to solve them, and (c) decide whether the sessions shall go on. In this first session the therapist might then ask the person to 'tell me about yourself'. The talk flows freely, but essentially in one direction: from the client to the psychologist, and directed by the client extensively. If the talk slows down, the therapist may repeat or rephrase a remark made by the client. If the patient has said 'I don't get along with my mates in the factory', it may be returned to him as 'You say you have personal difficulties on your job'. The tone used is deliberately neutral, implying neither approval nor disapproval.

Typically this non-directive technique leads to exploration of personal problems which contribute to unhappiness and ineffective behaviour. From that point the discussion moves off towards consideration of different behaviour responses or patterns of conduct which might be more satisfying. New reactions or attitudes may be tried out between sessions and reported back by the patient. The patient evaluates the effects of these different courses of action and their relative benefits. The treatment becomes a pattern: the problem is stated, various courses of action are considered, one is chosen and carried through. Later its efficiency is discussed and evaluated. In time the individual learns to deal with his own problems and no longer requires professional assistance. If successful, the therapist has induced the patient to clarify his problems, to find solutions to them, and to act on them successfully.

Summary

The disorders of mental health are the neuroses, which are ineffective acquired patterns of behaviour and are accompanied by feelings of anxiety, fear, guilt, etc., and the psychoses, both functional and organic, which are personality disturbances. The latter are normally treated by drugs and medications. The neuroses sometimes respond to therapy. Psychoanalysis and non-directive therapy were described as examples of psychotherapy. All therapies seem to depend on learning. They stimulate the patient to try *fresh* means to *wanted* ends.

FURTHER READING

Freud, S., *Introductory Lectures on Psychology* (1915–17), Hogarth, 1962

Hays, Peter, *New Horizons in Psychiatry*, Penguin, 1964

Lindner, R., *The Fifty Minute Hour*, Corgi (first published in the U.S.A., 1955)

McIver, J., *The Frog Pond*, New York, Braziller, 1963

CHAPTER THIRTEEN

PERSONALITY THEORY

We all try to understand each other's behaviour and want to know why people speak and act in their own characteristic ways. If the different topics in this book cover some of the parts, or causes, of our behaviour, and can be likened to the pieces of a jigsaw puzzle, then 'personality' can be called the completed puzzle.

There are many ideas about personality, and some of the ideas of men like Freud, Jung, and Adler are widely known. Concepts such as ego, extravert, introvert, and inferiority complex are in daily, if muddled, use.

Just as each person's fingerprints form a pattern unique to himself, so personality can be regarded as the combination of loops, lines, and marks identifying each of us. Personality theorists have been working hard to identify and label these traits which, like the loops, lines, and marks, are the basic dimensions upon which each person can be measured and identified.

In Aristotle's time, personality was described in relation to the predominance in each individual of the supposed basic body fluids. An individual's personality fell under one of these four categories:

Body fluid	*Personality type*
Warm blooded	Amiable and pleasant
Phlegmatic	Listless and slow
Black bile	Depressed and melancholic
Yellow bile	Easily angered and temperamental

These classifications assumed a relationship between the chemistry of the body and the nature of personality. Modern research has substantiated the relationship between the functioning of our glands and organs and the way in which we behave, but the results do not show as clear-cut a set of relationships as that suggested by Aristotle. Such a four-way classification system does not account for the great variability between persons and within one person.

In more recent times renewed efforts have been made to describe personality in terms of body types, but the types were determined from photographs of a large number of university students. The fat man (called an endomorph) was supposed to be a jolly, happy-go-lucky person. The thin man type (ectomorph) was supposed to be sensitive, withdrawn, and anxious. The muscular type (mesomorph) was supposed to be energetic and direct in his manner. Each type of person was supposed to have a personality structure reflecting his body type. When this scheme was subjected to careful review, however, the people who judged the body shapes were found also to have judged the personality attributes, which makes the material suspect.

Sigmund Freud, the founder of psychoanalysis, developed a number of unusual ideas about personality from his work as a psychiatrist with disturbed patients. Many of his patients were suffering from behaviour disorders which he found to be related to their experiences in childhood. Based upon these experiences in Vienna, Freud published his formulations about the development and structure of personality. One of the startling ideas that he called attention to was the suggestion that sexual needs *in childhood* are of crucial importance in the growth and development of adult behaviour. He emphasized the proposition that our actions are motivated almost exclusively by sexual drives. The idea that a child should desire sexual gratification as the adult knows it was at first, for Western society, absurd, and Freud was widely criticized. The major complaint and the subsequent misunderstanding revolved over the word 'sex'. In Freud's usage it apparently included not just the desires and needs associated with carnal sex, but all the basic drives, needs, and motives. As we know, the bodily needs such as food, shelter, avoidance of pain, and so on are fundamental drives activating and directing our behaviour. We cannot survive without minimum fulfilment of the drives, but sexual needs are probably of less importance. The misunderstanding was central and of major importance for Freud, his supporters, and his critics.

Freud divided personality structure into three parts. The *id* was conceived as an animal driving source which seeks immediate satisfaction of the basic, irrational, pleasure-seeking impulses. Children were described as creatures who are primarily governed in their behaviour by the forces from the id. The *ego* was proposed as a counter-force which governs the need for social approval. It directs our behaviour into socially acceptable patterns. At the opposite pole to the id is the *super-ego*, which is very much like conscience. This part of our personality is supposed to make us behave as our parents taught us and as we ideally think we should behave. The id and super-ego are supposed to be in conflict all the time, with the ego acting as a referee and mediator between the two. According to Freud, there are occasions when the id may gain the upper hand and dominate our behaviour; when, for example, someone inexplicably commits an improper act. There are other occasions when the super-ego controls behaviour, when we fight for ideals even though our livelihood and well-being are endangered.

Like many of the theories that preceded Freud's, his thesis oversimplifies the nature of personality. Important traits like intelligence are virtually ignored, and the nature of the basic drives is confused. The main benefit to psychology has been the exposition of the influence of the sexual needs, and the creation of a common language and point of view for many students of personality.

Another serious criticism of Freud is that he derived his ideas from work with mental patients and disturbed people. This is analagous to the mechanic who tries to understand the principles of the motor car by examining only wrecked vehicles. Many psychologists reject the Freudian approach because it is both subjective and ambiguous. Yet Freud was a major pioneer. Efforts are now being made to bring psychoanalytic theory to terms with the accumulated work in personality of the past few decades, and even those who disagree most violently with Freud find themselves using his language with which to reject him.

Other psychologists prefer to make a fresh start with a different language through concepts derived from the many studies of learning theory. Personality structure is described and examined in terms of the stimulus–response–reward–response patterns that are the habitual ways in which we conduct ourselves. Learning theories (described in earlier chapters), such as classical conditioning and operant conditioning, provide plausible models of the formation of personality. If behaviour and personality are reshaped by learning experiences then there is a legitimate approach to personality description through the approach made by learning theories.

The work of Raymond B. Cattell is probably the best of contemporary effort to identify the structure of personality. Cattell has performed a prodigious amount of research. He intiated his search for the dimensions of personality by first collecting and analysing various forms of data used to describe human behaviour. He studied verbal descriptions, man-to-man ratings, laboratory studies, and observations of people in their natural settings, all for the purpose of collecting an inclusive mass of data. From this accumulation of information he computed statistical indices of relationship between the many different characteristics described. These data were then put through a process of information-reduction called *factor analysis*. This statistical process of factor analysis, which could actually be performed only in recent times in most cases with the development of high-speed computers, treats the data in much the same way as heat affects different liquids in a distillation apparatus. As the 'heat' or analysis is applied, different factors with the same characteristics or 'boiling points' are successively 'boiled off' and collected. When the process is finished, the different traits or characteristics that were found to be the same are separately examined and identified. Cattell found that the common basic personality traits that seemed to be most descriptive of our different behaviours were the following (for clarity the trait names used here are slightly different from those used by Cattell):

A. Good-natured v. Aloof
B. Intelligent v. Dull
C. Mature v. Emotional
E. Assertive v. Submissive
F. Happy-go-lucky v. Sober
G. Conscientious v. Expedient
H. Adventuresome v. Timid and Shy
I. Realistically Tough v. Sensitive
L. Trusting v. Suspicious
M. Practical v. Imaginative
N. Shrewd v. Simply Kind
O. Self-confident v. Insecure and Anxious
Q1. Liberal v. Conservative
Q2. Self-sufficient v. Dependent
Q3. Self-controlled v. Unreliable
Q4. Relaxed v. Tense

NOTE: The above index letters coincide with the factors identified by Cattell.

This collection of personality traits is not the last word in the
analysis of personality structure. They do, however, serve as a
good approximation of the main personality indicators, as the
loops, lines, and marks do in fingerprinting. Further steps to-
ward development of reliable and valid measuring procedures
are still going on so that personality may be objectively assessed
without the need for ambiguous and unreliable subjectivity in
the basic assessment.

The psychologist nurtured in the tradition of objective in-
vestigation and reliable measurement is dismayed by the multitude of speculations about personality. There is a particular
confusion between what he would call psychology and psychoanalogy. In psychoanalogy a model or analogy is developed
which helps to describe what is being talked about. We could
use the motor car as a model for characterizing concepts in
psychology. The engine corresponds to our drives, the petrol
tank to our needs, and the brakes to our learned inhibitions.

The confusion occurs when we begin to treat the model as the real thing and start to insist that man acts just like a car. Any effort to define, identify, and understand the personality of man must be grounded in reliable terms of measurement, or else it will end up, as the rest have, on the rocky shores of ambiguity and subjectivity. Oversimplification is another malady that has afflicted personality theorists. Man is far too complex to be accounted for by just a few simple forces like id, ego, or the like.

Many of the past differences in theory come closer to resolution if we consider personality as if it were a structure, as we viewed intelligence, with different views or perspectives providing a different picture. Intelligence was described as being like a large container with different compartments corresponding to the many different abilities which compose the total individual characteristics of mental ability. In the same way personality can be likened perhaps to a mask. Each of the features of the mask, such as the eyes, ears, nose, mouth, etc., are like the different traits of the personality. The colour of the eyes, the size of the ears, the shape of the nose, etc., can be likened to the *degree* to which each of these traits are conspicuous features in an individual's personality. However limited this analogy is, we can readily see that personality can be observed and described, as we describe a face, in terms of a few prominent features or in the overall appearance.

The following broad, general features of characteristic traits of personality have been more recently found by Heron to be related. (Notice that the main headings represent more prominent and noticeable traits and the others listed below them have been found to be detailed parts of the overall feature or characteristic.)

General Emotional Stability

This trait (like one's eyes, which are noticeable) is a personality feature which captures our attention. Statistical research has shown that six of the traits listed by Cattell are highly related to this characteristic. The different parts of the eye, the eyelids, eyebrows, iris, etc., may be likened to the following, which seem to make up the overall behaviour trait of maturity or emotional stability.

C. Mature v. Emotional
L. Trusting v. Suspicious
M. Practical v. Imaginative
O. Self-confident v. Insecure and Anxious
Q3. Self-controlled v. Unreliable
Q4. Relaxed v. Tense

These can also be called, in Freud's terminology, 'ego-strength', which leads to some agreement among the different theories and the different theory languages. For a global assessment of personality, emotional stability might be measured. For more detailed understanding this trait would be more intensively examined in terms of self-confidence, tenseness, tendency to trust others, etc.

Extraversion–Introversion

These were the terms suggested by Jung and have been found to be highly related to Cattell's factors of :

A. Good-natured v. Aloof
E. Assertive v. Submissive
F. Happy-go-lucky v. Sober
H. Adventuresome v. Timid and Shy
Q2. Self-sufficient v. Dependent

Each of these subdivisions of extraversion–introversion again seem to be on a slightly different perspective of the same global, characteristic.

Tender-mindedness–Tough-mindedness

The traits that relate to this additional characteristic are :

N. Simply Kind v. Shrewd
I. Sensitive v. Realistically Tough

This trait is less well defined by the two parts described here, but the apparent similarity is still quite compelling. This similarity is also supported by statistical studies of the relationship between the different traits.

Radicalism–Conservatism

This trait has also been called liberalism–conservatism. Liberalism, in this sense, proposes the 'abolition of private property', while the opposite pole would be represented by the feeling that 'nationalism is inefficient'. It is obviously a social attitude characteristic of people, as in Tender-mindedness–Tough-mindedness. Factor Q1 defines this characteristic of personality.

Super-ego

This trait, perhaps better called moral values, seems to be the personality characteristic which governs the tendency to be a socially conforming, ethical, and moral individual in life. Cattell found this to be exhibited by a pattern of behaviour called conscientious *v.* expedient (G). People who are deficient in this trait are frivolous, immature, and neglectful of their social responsibilities.

Intelligence

This last trait (B) needs no description here as it is a universally accepted feature of personality which we have described in detail in a previous chapter. It is included as a trait of personality because it appears in virtually all of the many studies of individual character and temperament.

These general traits of emotional stability, extraversion–introversion, tender-mindedness–tough-mindedness, radicalism–conservatism, super-ego, and intelligence are not offered as the final word on the relationship of the basic traits of human behaviour. They do, however, represent an attempt to bring together many of the different trait names and temperament characteristics into a more rational whole. If we conceptualize them as analagous to the more prominent features of a mask, perhaps we come a little closer to a visual picture of personality structure.

Summary

The theories of Freud, Jung, and other psychologists present some of the complexities of trying to obtain an understanding of an individual's unique personality development and structure. Six general personality traits were listed as broad general personality characteristics, and the other traits were subsumed as subdivisions of these traits.

FURTHER READING

Cattell, R. B., *The Scientific Analysis of Personality*, Penguin, 1965
Brown, J. A. C., *Freud and the Post-Freudians*, Penguin, 1961

CHAPTER FOURTEEN

MEASURING PERSONALITY

THERE are a number of technical problems that must be faced when a psychologist sets out to measure the unique features of a person's behaviour which characterizes his individuality. The first difficulty is the very concept with which he is dealing. Personality can be thought of as a dynamic, changing, 'fluid' kind of structure which is always in some state of movement. It is indeed a sufficiently vague concept to allow only a tenuous kind of grip for measurement to be placed on it. If certain features are found to be sufficiently stable and constant, then some reliable measurement can be made.

The next problem is to devise a measuring technique which is so standardized that it can be administered by all of the people who have been trained to do so. Such procedures must be standardized for administration, scoring, and interpretation, so that the ambiguities of personality measurement are kept to the minimum. The personal element is another one of the perplexing problems in personality measurement. Many methods and techniques of personality assessment require some individual influence upon the administration of the test, scoring of the responses, and interpretation of the meaning of the responses. The assessor can try to behave objectively, but he can never be completely removed. Any unusual orientation or action on the part of the assessor thereby contaminates the results of the measurement and data collection.

If all of these problems were to be resolved successfully, an added difficulty is found in the requirement for classification of the responses. Unlike the kinds of items found in intelligence or ability tests, where there is almost complete agreement among the experts and the layman as to what constitutes the right answer, in personality assessment the proper answer is usually the 'typical' response, about which there is less than unanimous agreement. This means that what is a 'good' answer is one that is expressed by the typical person, and extreme answers, by definition, characterize the unusual person. In ability testing, the respondent tries to obtain a *correct* answer; in personality assessment, his goal is usually to achieve the *typical* answer. Because of this difference of correct–incorrect response in tests, where it is a matter of 'black and white', and degree of desirability in personality assessment, the concept 'test' is usually reserved for ability testing only. Personality measurements are more appropriately described as measurement and assessment techniques, not as tests.

Behaviour

One way to measure personality is to take a sampling of behaviour. This sample may be obtained by direct observation of action in the natural setting, or it may be obtained in certain contrived situations. The assessor establishes conditions which are standardized so that he can compare the actions of different people, and he focuses his attention and culls out those which are most revealing.

One way to sample behaviour, and probably the one most frequently employed, is the personal interview. Employment officers, social workers, job supervisors, and the housewife hiring her 'daily help', all employ the interview method in an effort to assess the nature of the personality and the potential success of the person they are talking to. The interview is properly defined as a 'purposeful conversation' intended to obtain information about a person's present and past behaviour for the purpose of predicting his future behaviour. There are many kinds of interviews, but the most common is the casual conversation where the interviewer does most of the talking, limiting the amount of information collected and available for evaluation. Statistical analysis of recorded interviews revealed that the greater proportion of time spent talking (by the interviewer) the less effective the interview. The most successful interview is one in which both parties talk about half the time. This is best accomplished by deliberate effort on the part of the interviewer; a skill developed through training. Good interviewers are as much made as born.

Another type of interview is the patterned interview where the conversation is focused upon specific, predetermined areas and topics of discussion. The interviewer works from a checklist which he uses as a guide and upon which he can, immediately after, enter his observations and evaluation before they are forgotten or modified by memory. Specific topics covered may include appearance, interests, previous work experience, and other topics reflecting maturity, emotional stability, and so on.

A third type is the non-directive interview, which is characterized by the single question 'tell me about yourself'. The interviewee is encouraged to talk as long and over as wide a range of topics as he chooses. The interviewer encourages with suitable comments. Also the listener may repeat a statement made earlier by the person, paraphasing it to make it seem like a new statement or question. If the last comment was 'I never got along with the others in school', the interviewer may reflect this back with a neutral-sounding remark like 'your social relationships with the people in school were ineffective'. Care is exercised so that the reflected comment is neither approving nor disapproving. Such a remark might create too much *structure* to the conversation, and the objective is to encourage the other man to make the choice of topic. This technique sounds much simpler than it actually is, and it requires a great deal of practice to be able to achieve it effectively. Some modern-day therapists employ this conversation technique in their therapy sessions.

Out of the experiences of personnel selection employed during the Second World War, personality assessors have learned to use a new technique. This interview technique is called the stress interview, and involves the use of different means for the induction of stress or distress. It is intended to bring out the characteristic defence mechanisms that a person employs when he encounters difficulty in his personal relationships. Stress is created by interruptions in the middle of a conversation – interruptions by the interviewer himself. This disturbing influence is achieved by direct or indirect criticisms of something said, by not letting the other man finish his comments before putting another query to him, or by stony silence. Not all people can successfully adapt to these conditions and blurt out remarks which they had no intention of making in the interview. This device must obviously be used with caution because someone can be seriously upset by the stress experience and become aggrieved against the interviewer and the sponsor of the interview. The disturbance is usually relieved by giving a full explanation to the interviewee before the session is over, so no harm will be done. Most people, after being driven some distance 'up the wall', are let down safely. (The non-directive interview serves well here.) The stress method *seems* to be ideal for the assessment of characteristic patterns of reaction to stress and should, in theory, reveal what adjustment mechanisms are employed under stress. Unfortunately, like many a promising technique, this one has been found wanting. In a careful study of the effects of stress interviewing of people applying for work and their subsequent adjustment to the jobs, no relationship was found. Stress interviews may be of some limited help, when employed by skilled people, and the method may bring out some useful but limited information, but this information can be obtained by other means which are less painful to both the interviewer and the interviewee.

Because interviews are tedious, time-consuming, and expensive, some people have found it useful to conduct group interviews. This method can only be utilized in the rare cases where the particular patterns of personality being searched for and examined are those which can be elicited in social situations. The guise of the interview may be a group discussion where the members are supposed to be solving a problem. The people exchanging information together can be evaluated on how they interact. The kinds of spontaneous remarks made in such group activities are likely to be indicative of personality traits. Also, since the others are doing the talking, the interviewer has more time available to observe and evaluate the different people in action. One of the limitations to this method is the fact that the members may defer to one particular member, because of age, social class, accent, etc. Another limitation is that one dominating person may make it impossible for the others to share the communication. This sampling process can be very useful if sufficient information is obtained about each individual.

A different sub-class of personality assessment techniques is the behaviour sample in situational role-playing sessions, or stress tests. Here the person being assessed is placed in a situation that may or may not resemble the tasks he will be required to face in life. He may be asked to play the role of an irate father, or a rebellious son. The way the man chooses to play the part, and the personality traits that are expressed by the choice of words and actions utilized, are entirely up to the actor. Obviously the way we choose to play our roles reveals attitudes and behaviour, and our unique pattern of adjustment to our environment.

Another source of behavioural information is the case-history method. The reader will remember that the case-history method was mentioned in Chapter 1, as one of the methods or techniques of science used by psychologists. This is a matter of collecting information about a person's past. The rationale for this method assumes that the nature of a person's choices in past life and the structure of his past environment will shape the pattern of behaviour he develops. Although this information could be gathered by research, it can often be obtained by straightforward inquiry. Consider the value, for instance, of 'birth order' as a case-history item. People who were brought up as the eldest of three in a family will be inclined to have a personality pattern showing greater sense of responsibility or 'super-ego'. This develops out of early and repeated experience of having to help bring up the younger sisters or brothers. The youngest of the large family often develops a reaction pattern suggesting the phrase 'spoiled brat'. Of course it would be foolish to generalize about personality on the basis of only one or two of these bits of information, but it has been found that a large number of these items, in combination, can approach reliability and predictability. Another illustration of the effectiveness of this approach is the fact that the number of creative discoveries made by scientists is highly related to the individual scientist's view of himself. Most researchers who have been awarded patents or submitted worthwhile discoveries in research and are judged as the more creative are found to think very highly of themselves (ego). This is not a result of the recognition they receive but seems to be a basic view of life. It is a characteristic personality trait that has been discovered both in England and in the U.S.A. Patent-holders tend to be self-centred. (There are exceptions, of course; but once again, it is not the single, isolated item which gives the accurate picture of personality but the aggregate of information.) There are other techniques for assessing personality through behaviour sampling, but those listed give the reader a representative picture.

Ratings

Personality assessment may also be achieved by a systematic rating procedure. In the usual rating scheme, a check-list is reviewed and the person being evaluated is judged and checks made on the characteristics listed. He is judged by someone who either is familiar with his behaviour or develops a picture of it by talking to him and observing his reactions. The list includes a variety of traits which have been selected as most relevant to the sponsor of the scheme. A rating scale (composed of three facets) for the trait of 'determination' might look like this:

Determination

1. outstanding   exceptional   very good   average
   below average   poor
2. gives up easily   usually finishes his tasks
   pushes on no matter what
3. seldom determined   occasionally determined
   always determined

The rating scale, most often used in industry for the evaluation of worker-performance and personal qualities, is filled out by the man's work supervisor, but in limited situations may be filled out by associates at the same level of responsibility, or even by those whom he supervises. The objective, in all cases, is to have judgements made by people who are sufficiently well informed and can therefore accurately assess behaviour and personality. This man-to-man rating scheme has a number of faults, the main one being that the judges tend to be lenient and generous in their ratings; i.e. 'everyone is good'. Also the rater will look at only one of the man's qualities and judge all of his temperament on the basis of that one trait. Finally, there is a tendency to discriminate among a few of the traits and not all of them. To use rating scales in a meaningful manner raters must be trained, and the results of the ratings must be judged against other standards and evidence of behaviour to show whether they are doing the task they are intended to perform. (Ratings would have to be compared to determine their validity.) In addition to the graphic type of rating scale illustrated, personality qualities may be judged among a group of people by other methods such as a ranking of men on one trait at a time, or by other types of check lists.

Questionnaire—Closed-end Responses

The most standardized form of personality assessment is the published questionnaire. These printed forms are usually filled out by the person himself and therefore constitute self-ratings. The questions take the following form (again the trait of 'determination' is the one being assesssed):

Do you consider yourself to be a determined person?
                                        yes. .... no. ....
Do other people regard you as being determined?
                                        yes. .... no. ....

Notice that the usual response categories are yes or no. These closed-end questionnaires restrict the dimensions of personality that are measured, as many people prefer to respond by 'in certain circumstances I behave in one way, and in others perhaps differently'. Which way is one to be oriented when filling out questionnaires? The central problems here are the transparency of the questions in the scale and the limitation of responses allowed. If the respondent is filling out this trait inventory as part of a job application process, he can easily fake his responses and portray virtually any personality profile which will help him achieve his goal. On the other hand, when these questionnaires are used in what is called 'guidance situations', where the respondent is sincerely interested in obtaining psychological assistance and guidance, the individual does supply authentic responses about himself. In all applications of the self-evaluation methods, these responses are limited by the unconscious biases that we have about ourselves. What kind of personality structure we *think* we have may be quite different from the structure recognized by others.

Despite these limitations, the closed-end questionnaire has been found to be a useful instrument for the assessment of personality if, as with all tools, it is intelligently used. Most advantageously, standards can be obtained; the typical response can be determined among the general population; and the responses can be interpreted in terms of statistical designations of normality.

It is essential to consider the following points in constructing a questionnaire: (a) variety in the response categories; (b) clarity in the wording of the questions; (c) the ordering of response categories in multiple-choice format, and (d) arranging the response choices into a format called 'forced-choice'. This latter type of questionnaire typically has four statements of behaviour, all of which may appear to be equally favourable or socially desirable. The difference in the questionnaire is that only two of the items are related to some outside standard of behaviour such as adjustment, and the other two may be most frequently chosen by people who are less well adjusted. Research on this format has revealed a major reduction in the fakeability or transparency of questionnaires, but it has not been completely eliminated. To avoid these restrictions and problems, many psychologists prefer to assess personality by the techniques that we discuss next.

Projective Devices

These techniques involve the use of various kinds of ambiguous stimuli like pictures of clouds, ink blots, etc. Since the material is essentially without clear content, the things that the respondent 'sees' and reports are a reflection of his own perceptions and the motives which drive and direct his behaviour. The pictures are called 'projective' because he projects himself, so to speak, into the situations which are suggested by the stimuli. The best-known and the most frequently used device in this category is the Rorschach set of ten standardized ink blots. The individual is shown one at a time and is asked 'What is this?' or 'What do you see?' (The obvious answer 'I see an ink blot' is interpreted as an indication of blocking and a reluctance to reveal the images which are perceived by the individual being assessed. He is advised to report what else he sees.) Responses are scored in terms of the total number of items seen, the types of items, whether they are animal, human, or inanimate objects, and so on. Also considered is whether the responses are based upon the whole ink blot or only a part of it. The psychologist interprets the responses subjectively, and he requires a great deal of experience with this instrument, common sense, insight, and ingenuity to obtain an accurate picture of personality. Projective devices have been notoriously abused, as a result of a failure to be sufficiently careful.

Another technique that has shown promise is one which uses a series of pictures depicting people in various situations. The respondent is requested to tell a story about the people in each picture. Because each person is liable to interpret the pictures differently, the psychologists claim that the responses, as raw material, may give a great deal of information into one's personality and dynamics of behaviour. Other projective devices which have been developed include the pictures of clouds or stick figures in different postures, and such techniques as having the person draw a picture of a man, a house, a tree, and so on. The crucial element in the use of projective, ambiguous stimuli is not the stimuli, or the exact responses, but the subjective, intuitive interpretation of the whole pattern of responses. In the hands of a skilled personality analyst, these projective methods, utilized as interview aids, can be useful tools for the exploration of personality.

Sentence Completion

One way to bridge the gap between the projective devices, which are ambiguously-formed stimuli, and the questionnaires, rating forms, and behaviour tests, which confine or retrict responses, is to use sentence completion procedure. The individual completes a series of sentences which are only partly made up, such as the following:

The thing that bothers me most..................................

I wish...

Mother..

This technique incorporates the desirable features of the projective techniques in that it is sufficiently ambiguous, that each respondent chooses the quality of response, and that it is appropriate for him and probably characteristic of his personality dynamics. This method also has the advantage of being sufficiently restricted so that responses can be more accurately scored and compared with the kinds of responses provided by representative populations. Like all the methods of personality assessment, this method also requires extensive trial, development, analysis, and interpretation. It is a method, however, which represents an attempt to achieve precision of measurement, and at the same time does not restrict the individual to choose one of two responses.

One of the major controversies between the proponents of the quantitive, objective methods of personality assessment and the advocates of the projective methods is the extent to which personality is being assessed 'on the surface' or whether 'depth of personality dynamics' are being reflected. The ultimate answer can only be obtained by extensive, systematic research and follow-up studies. These studies are being performed and published, and the psychologist who can manage to keep up with the volume of published material on personality is achieving a major task.

Probably the only accurate assessment of the personality of the 'whole man' will come from a new combination of the techniques described.

Summary

Personality is a difficult and complicated process to be measured, but many different approaches can be utilized to construct a picture of an individual's unique patterns of behaviour. These methods include the sampling of behaviour through different interview procedures, stress tests, life-history analysis, closed and open-ended questionnaires, and projective techniques. A combined approach is probably the most useful.

FURTHER READING

Vernon, P. E., *Personality Assessments*, Methuen, 1964

Eysenck, H. J., *The Structure of Human Personality* (2nd edition), Methuen, 1960

CHAPTER FIFTEEN

INDUSTRIAL PSYCHOLOGY

INDUSTRIAL psychology is broadly defined as the application of psychology to the problems of business and industry. Industrial psychologists (a) try to find the most effective ways to select the successful people, (b) develop procedures for placing them in the job in which they will be most likely to succeed, (c) train them to perform their work in a satisfactory manner, (d) devise methods for measuring and evaluating the workers' performance, (e) investigate the effects of different kinds of working conditions and recommend changes which will result in an increase in both production and worker satisfaction, (f) design more effective equipment for use by the worker with a minimum of error, and (g) study advertisements to help develop a campaign to improve sales. Short of sweeping up after the office staff has gone home for the night, the industrial psychologist tends to find himself involved in virtually all problems in industry.

We are accustomed to think of industrial psychologists being employed in the selection of candidates for employment but it is equally important that workers should be happy in their work and be given opportunity and encouragement to produce their best efforts. The psychologist in industry helps fit the worker to the job by scientific methods of selection, placement, training, and by performance evaluation. He also helps fit the job to the worker through work analysis, ergonomics, and human-relations study.

Selection and Testing

High costs of production, the expense of training help, the expense due to misuse of machinery, the losses due to absenteeism, illness, accidents, and so on have all contributed to the demand for methods which will lead to good staff. No ideal method exists, but a systematic process of selection is significantly more reliable than an unsystematic one. The psychologist may choose a series of tests to measure aptitude, intelligence, manual dexterity, technical competence, clerical ability, personality, interests, special skills, or whatever is found to be important to job success. The application form may also be examined and scored. Marks are awarded for various attributes which have been found, through empirical study, to identify better employees. A systematic interview will also supply useful information about an applicant for employment but the interview is only a blunt, primitive 'tool'. It is not as precise or reliable as a well constructed, validated test. Most interviews are simply conversations between applicant and employer in which each can evaluate the other. Information regarding work experience is usually obtained and the interviewer advises on the requirements and opportunities within the sponsoring company. The success of the interview depends, in the last analysis, upon the methods and powers of judgement used to evaluate work potential.

Placement includes the interpretation of employment information so that the 'right man' is placed on the 'right job'. Placement also includes designation of the most suitable candidate to be promoted to the level where both he and the company approach maximum benefit. Additional testing, including the administration of interest inventories, personality questionnaires, and other interviews may be used.

Training

For most large industries, new employees are like raw materials ready for the industrial process to transform them before they can be effective 'products'. A new worker who is put to work without special training is apt to be unsatisfacory to the company and to himself. He cannot know how he is expected to perform his job, what are local procedures, the channels of communication and supervision, the customs of the 'industrial village' in which he is a new resident. Training in industry is essential in most companies, whether they are large production organizations with thousands on the staff, or small family concerns with just a few employees. In the earlier days of industry, and even among the small firms today, the general practice was to have the new worker 'sit by Nellie' in order to learn the job. This does not really work very well, although it would seem to be the easiest and cheapest. 'Nellie' is not a qualified instructor, in most instances, although she may be a reliable, skilled worker. Very often she has little of the skill, knowledge, or attitudes necessary to help a new worker become a productive member of an industrial organization. The answer that serves most employers is to have a systematic training programme. This programme will include orientation training to introduce the worker to his mates and to help him learn how he fits into the overall organization. If the type of work is one which the worker has never performed before, a very extensive training programme may be required in which the trainee is given intensive instruction in and practice of the skills and activities. In this way, errors which could be expensive or dangerous are avoided. It has been found repeatedly in industry that pre-training is the cheapest method for bringing new workers up to maximum levels of skill in the minimum time. Some training programmes are a few hours' duration; others, a few days or weeks; some go on for years. These programmes may incorporate classroom teaching and on-the-job training. The student 'earns while he learns'.

There are some training programmes for the teaching of

management skills, but these are experimental in most cases as the results are difficult to evaluate.

Performance Evaluation

Granted the employer knows how to select, place, and train the new worker, he still needs to evaluate his effectiveness. Work performance is evaluated in many different ways in different organizations. If a man is to be promoted, transferred, or discharged, management must have reliable information upon which to make its decisions. In the absence of reliable data, rumour or prejudice are expensive second choices. A periodic and reliable evaluation of each man's work performance is one way of avoiding overall inefficiency, discontent, and excessive costs. A frequent method for performance evaluation is to have the immediate supervisor who has personal knowledge of the workers' daily performance prepare a rating form or check list. This is very much like the forms utilized for personality assessment, except that work not personality characteristics is identified and rated. Statistical analysis of many different performance evaluation procedures has revealed that most supervisors basically evaluate three aspects of behaviour on the job: quality of work, quantity of work, and what is (vaguely) called 'compassion'. This last trait is usually a personality trait that permeates most performance evaluations and reflects the personal qualities of the man being rated and his perceived potential for promotion. Other traits listed on performance evaluation forms tend to be biased by the judgements about these three basic traits.

To simplify worker evaluation, some organizations have the worker rated simply as 'satisfacory', 'outstanding', or 'unsatisfactory'. The majority of workers receive the first category, and no further data are needed. When an employee is described as outstanding (implying that he is entitled to a rise) or unsatisfactory (implying that he should be discharged) specific justification and support is requested to demonstrate that the judgement is not an arbitrary one but is based upon reliable evidence.

The simplest technique of performance evaluation is the ranking method, where each worker in the shop is ranked by his supervisor. This requires clear-cut decisions by the supervisor regarding the relative merits of each man in the shop. It may be an excellent method for obtaining discriminations as the supervisor is usually reluctant to criticize someone's performance; he often wishes to assign descriptions of outstanding performance to everybody, which negates other procedures.

Other methods, too complicated to be described here, may be used to evaluate the performance of the workers, but what must be emphasized is the role the psychologist plays in industry. He helps to develop a rating form for the organization, he trains the supervisors in its proper use, he prepares reliable methods for analysis of the data of worker performance. The psychologist brings to industry the benefits of scientific method, reducing the unreliability – and costs – of 'common sense'.

Working Conditions

One of the more confusing problems in industrial psychology is the importance of working conditions. Some organizations are found to have maximum production in unsuitable physical environments. Some, with modern facilities, the latest machines, noise control, background music, etc., are described by their employees as dull, cold mausoleums, and production is low and costly. The issue is most often resolved in terms of the overall attitude of management towards the workers and staff. If the management is considerate of its staff, then, it appears, almost anything else goes. If the supervisors are excessively interested in getting the work out, and are indifferent to human considerations, then one will expect grievances, accidents, absences, illness, poor quality of work, and excessive waste. What is required in the way of decent working conditions is (at least) the minimum arrangements that physically allow the work to be accomplished. This means adequate lighting, heating, ventilation, noise proofing, and the appropriate design of work places.

Ergonomics

This term refers to the effective design of machines for efficient human operation. Human engineering, as it is sometimes called, involves the study of the dialogue between man and machine. The most effective operation between the two is a matter of a machine properly designed for operation by its human controller. The principles of man-machine systems are based upon past experience in most instances, and the modification of machines for effective human operation is usually decided upon after detailed analysis of its experience. With the advent in the last few decades of many new machines, and the problems of designing space vehicles and military weapons, engineers are required to know more about the capabilities and limitations of man. Errors in design may cost millions of pounds. At one time when designers had to cope with the problem of designing an automobile seat to be sat in by people of varying sizes and shapes, weights and girths, error in design might only discomfort the driver. The correct design of the seat and cockpit of a modern airliner, however, is a matter of life and death to the passengers, as the first 'misunderstanding' between the pilot and his machine can be fatal. Common sense has been found to be limited in many man-machine problems. Consider, for instance, the problem of noise and vocal communication. How do you improve the understanding of conversation on a very noisy factory floor? Common sense tells us to improve hearing ability, perhaps by giving the men hearing aids. Unfortunately, all these do is make it even more difficult. The correct solution is to put in ear plugs! The understanding of conversation in a noisy atmosphere is improved only if the ratio of speech to noise is changed, and the simple expedient of partially plugging up the ears works wonders.

Psychologists who are employed in the task of improving machines, equipment, work arrangements, and even work areas usually look into the situation in terms of the processes of:

Information on presentation: the design of dial displays and other sensory stimuli which are intended to communicate information to the operator.

Decision-making: the choice of sense modalities and equipment features which are most likely to lead to accurate interpretation. A bell for a telephone seems the best way of alerting the receiver of the call. A traffic signal is better understood if it is seen, not heard, because engine noise would mask it.

Performance: the correct design of the equipment so that action and machine reaction are in harmony. If a lever activates a punch press, the direction of movement of the lever should be in harmony with the press. Up lever – up goes the press.

By this approach to the man-machine communication and interaction process, the human engineer will identify operation problems and try out various alternative designs to see which one meets desired standards. The acceptance of curved-back chairs in today's schools is a triumph of human engineering over the persistence of the manufacturers in selling equipment that was standard but inefficient. It has taken us a long time to recognize that we are not a people with square bottoms and flat backs.

In addition to the types of activities listed above, the psychologist employed by business or industry performs work analysis and work methods improvements. He studies development of wage and salary evaluation systems to obtain equitable compensation schemes. Also, he may investigate the causes of accidents, the techniques of inspection, and other psychological conditions which contribute to efficiency and productivity. Finally, we find the broad area of human relations which involves the atmosphere of employment in which workers and management are in harmony.

Industrial harmony is difficult to establish and maintain because the needs and desires of management and the workers are not identical. Employers want a high level of productivity and profitability; workers desire satisfaction of their individual and group needs. There is no simple, direct relationship between productivity and morale but a variety of working arrangements and benefits seems essential for mutual satisfaction. The primary goals of one worker may be a high salary and good prospects for advancement; for a second person the goals may be work stability and job security; for a third, group acceptance and popularity. A narrow, inflexible personnel policy disregards the variable nature of working people.

Research into worker needs and motives has shown that they are the same as those of other 'types' of people, but a few generalizations are appropriate. For example, the higher the skill level, the greater the job satisfaction. A democratic style of supervision is preferred to an autocratic one, but ambiguity and inconsistency is the least preferred work environment. Employees wish to be recognized and treated as the unique individuals that they are, not as cogs in a machine. Only when there is a climate of mutual consideration can there be industrial harmony.

Summary

Psychology in industry is usually applied to selection, placement, training, performance evaluation, equipment design, working conditions, and other business and personnel problems.

FURTHER READING

Tiffin, J., and McCormick, E., *Industrial Psychology* (5th edition), New Jersey, Prentice-Hall, 1965

Lawshe, C. H., and Balma, M. J., *Principles of Personnel Testing* (2nd edition), McGraw-Hill, 1966

CHAPTER SIXTEEN

FRONTIERS IN PSYCHOLOGY

PSYCHOLOGY has come a long way since its early days of speculation, introspection, and uncontrolled experimentation. Theories that are published today are often the products of many years of data accumulation and analysis, and high-speed computers have become an important tool to the psychologist. Biologists, physicians, chemists, and engineers all use data supplied by the psychologist. The discovery and testing of new drugs for the treatment of behaviour disturbances is just one area where the cooperation of the different disciplines has helped man to handle his environment. The engineer who is designing automobile seats, highway signs, or industrial machines gets better results when he works in conjunction with psychologists who are aware of the characteristics of the potential user. It may be interesting to concentrate in this final chapter upon a few of psychology's newer activities.

Teaching machines are one of the practical applications of certain principles of the process of education. The name 'teaching machine' has, in the past twenty-five years, become a symbol for a type of teaching aid that is quite different from anything that has been developed in the educational scene. Broadly speaking, the teaching machine can be likened to individual tutoring, in contrast to other educational devices which are more like the traditional school lesson. In fact, the word 'machine' is not really essential to describe this revolutionary phenomenon. The more precise generic title is 'programmed learning'. Programmed learning materials are built into the machine in a prearranged teaching plan, but they may also be offered in a book or any other way where relatively small steps of information can be presented to the student.

First of all, let us consider what is called the *linear* method of programmed learning. The student is presented with a question or statement and is required to respond to it by writing what he thinks is the correct answer. If he has made a successful choice then he is presented with the next item of information. He again responds, and so on through the programme until he has mastered it. The special features of programmed learning material are listed below.

1. The presentation of material in small units.
2. Arrangements of material so that each item or frame is successfully mastered by ninety-five per cent of the students who attempt it for the first time.

3. Active participation by the student in the learning process, rather than the more passive activity of listening to a lecture or reading a book.

4. Immediate knowledge of results. Unlike the other learning experiences, the student discovers immediately whether he has learned the preceding bit of information or his learning efforts were too superficial.

5. Each student proceeds at his own rate of learning. The quick ones move ahead without being held back; the slow learner can also learn at the rate which will give him mastery of the material.

The second type of programmed learning is called branching or intrinsic programming. Here, instead of the direct question-and-answer technique (with or without the need for actually *writing* answer to questions), we have the multiple-choice question as the basis. A question is asked in the following manner:

If $x = 3$ and $y = 4$
what is the value of $x^2 + y^2$?

And this question may be followed by a set of alternative answers, such as

1. 7
2. 13
3. 25
4. 19

where the student is asked to choose the correct answer, or the student is asked to think or write his own answer first, and then turn to another frame (page) of the programme, where the set of alternative answers is presented.

Wrong answers selected in the multiple-choice situation may lead to a further explanation and analysis followed by further questions, until the correct answer is made.

Recent research shows that people can be taught virtually *any* subject by these methods of programmed instruction. The special advantage in the use of the teaching machine is *not* that teachers can be replaced and the costs of public education reduced. The programmed material is an aid to instruction, not a substitute for other means. The teacher who uses this material finds that his efforts are devoted less to trying to communicate rudiments and fundamentals of the subject matter, which in the classroom means reading aloud the textbook to the students. The teacher becomes a more valuable and resourceful person who serves as a discussion leader and helps the students understand and relate the material to other fields of interest and other facts of life not included in the text or programme.

All this means that our existing educational system will have to be completely rethought around the teaching machine, as well as to a lesser extent around other audio-visual aids.

Cybernetics

In the last twenty years, a new aspect of behavioural and biological studies has grown up, which is directly relevant to psychology. This new aspect of science is called *cybernetics*, and it was defined by Norbert Wiener as the science of control and communication in animals and men. The main object of cybernetics is to provide *effective* models of the human thinking processes, any other aspects of biological systems, or indeed of any system at all.

We can divide the problems that come under the heading of cybernetics into roughly three categories. The first category is that of simulating intelligence artificially, with devices as extensive as human intelligence or more so. The second class is concerned with the development of models which are explicit mechanical representations of human behaviour. In other words an attempt is being made explicitly to introduce the same principles into the machines as were observable in the human beings, or in animals. There is a third category of cybernetic problems which actually tries to construct the models in a similar fabric to that of humans and other organisms, but this is largely in the future, in the fields of physiology, chemistry, and allied subjects. We shall not be discussing this third category of cybernetic problem at all.

In short, cybernetics is concerned with artificial intelligence. It is certainly concerned with other things besides, and we can quickly draw attention to what earmarks a cybernetic approach to a problem. A cybernetic model is above all *effective*. By effective, we mean that it supplies a theory in a blueprint form, such that a machine in hardware could immediately be built from the blueprint. Alternatively, from the blueprint could be built a computer programme which would be known actually to work when put on the computer. What would not be tolerated by a cybernetic modelling system is the vagueness of ordinary language which would leave everyone in doubt as to what was specifically intended by a verbal description which was non-effective. In other words the test of the cybernetic model is that it is effectively constructable.

The methods that have been used by cyberneticians could be divided up into those of 'hardware' and those of 'software'. The hardware models include models of small organisms, such as the tortoise of Grey Walter and the maze runner of Shannon, right up to hardware models of the nervous system of the eye and the ear, and so on. On the software side of cybernetic development, we have digital computer programmes, the development of infinite automata, the development of information theory, and other statistical methods. Mathematics plays a very large part in the development of cybernetic models, and indeed some part of the origin of cybernetics goes back to mathematics and the association between the development of mathematics and the design of digital computers.

It was David Hilbert, the German mathematician, who first asked whether the whole of mathematics could be reproduced on a purely *machine-like* basis. In other words, he wanted to know whether mathematical proofs, or the decision as to whether a statement was a provable statement or not within the domain of classical mathematics, could be produced on a machine-like basis. This required some sort of definition of what was meant by the word 'machine-like'. It was suggested that a suitable definition would be that of a *decision procedure*. Decision procedures are affective techniques which require no insight or intelligence on the part of the person performing the procedures. The person needs neither a knowledge of the purpose for which the procedure is being performed, nor a knowledge of the detailed methods. An example of this is that of searching through the telephone directory to find out all the people in the directory who have their telephone on a particular exchange. All the person who is searching has to do is to assign a mark against each person on the exchange. The total of marks represents the total number of people on the exchange.

The idea of a decision procedure was originally something which was intended to convey what could be done by digital computer. Indeed, as a result of this sort of research, it was discovered that the whole of mathematics could not be so processed. There is a creative aspect to mathematics which if simulated by machine would entail the possibility of a number of wrong results. This leads many people into thinking that cybernetics could never produce, artificially, a system with the same degree of complexity and intelligence as a human system. This conclusion is false because of course the decision procedure definition is too narrow to encompass the whole of what can be done by machine. In short it is 'machine-like' in the sense of a traditional type of machine which is purely passive, but does not in any sense convey what can be made artificially, that is a machine which is self adapting and can learn from experience.

The problem of cybernetics then becomes how to produce the 'creative ability' and the general problem-solving activity which is so manifestly a part of human behaviour. The answer is, as with humans, that there can be no way of providing this artificially other than on a probability basis. In other words, humans and machines, which have to formulate generalizations, or heuristics as they are sometimes called, must be liable to make errors.

The procedure followed is very similar to the procedure in constructing scientific theories. In constructing scientific theories, or models, we proceed by systematic observation, from which we derive inductive generalizations. These inductive generalizations are the basis for deductive inference which in turn lead to further observations to check by coherence and consistency, as well as by direct confirmation through observation, the validity of the statements so derived. In other words it is rather as if the deductive status of the operation were machine-like in the first sense of the term 'machine-like'. By that we can extend the word machine-like to include inductive as well as deductive operations, and this can only be done by generalizing on a certain finite number of instances.

As soon as we argue from the particular to the general, so that we say given 1, 2, 3, etc. instances of the general class, then all members of the class have that particular characteristic, we stand in the need of doing one or two possible things. The first thing is to extend, or restrict further in the light of further experience, the defining characteristics of the class. The alternative is to redefine the classes in such a way that they are consistent with information still not available at the time the original class definitions were set out. Either way you look at it, the position is that at any particular time you cannot always know what future information has in store for you, and hence the categories of classes set up at any instance may turn out to be inadequate in the light of further evidence. This procedure is obviously a part of what is entailed in mathematics, or any empirical science. It is, however, clear that in terms of empirical science or mathematical development, there is no reason to doubt the ability of the machine to perform these further operations.

We described earlier the processes of sensation, perception, recognition, memory, thinking, problem solving, learning, and motor activity. There are a whole range of cognitive activities which we have described in this book, and our problem in the limit would be to show how these could all be modelled together in one hardware system. We say hardware system, but in fact, of course, an effective software system would be sufficient for our purpose and satisfy the cybernetic requirements.

A large number of models have been suggested already for perception. Classification models, specific sensory systems capable of being produced in hardware, such as those developed by Professor J. T. Culbertson (1952) and Professors McCulloch and Pitts (1947), are examples of the sort of system we have in mind. These classify information at the input end and sort it out into stages which allow the brain to make a decision in the light of all the information classified in the terms of all the different sensory inputs.

In fact we can say that there already exist many different models of perception, learning, thinking, problem solving, and language, as they occur in human behaviour. We shall not follow up the details of these models, but models in all these fields actually exist in software, hardware, or both.

In a sense these cybernetic models are designed to remove the vagueness that exists in ordinary scientific models whenever ordinary language is used (in other words, this is a problem of semantics).

One product of cybernetic research is decision taking, and we may expect international affairs and international tensions to be eased by what some people have called 'peace psychology'. This is really a part of the development of modern social psychology, which allows for a closer analysis of how corporate decisions are taken. It has been suggested that an international social model could now be constructed on a complex feedback basis, which would allow us to understand more completely the nature of international quarrels and thus enable us to control them.

The future in psychological research should bring forth much more information about human behaviour. With that information perhaps we may also gain greater understanding of our conduct and action, and this new-gained insight could teach us how to make the world a better place in which to live.

Summary

Many new frontiers are being explored in psychology today. We have looked at teaching machines and the study of cybernetics. Models of different features of human behaviour are being developed as a stimulus for greater insight into the dynamics of human performance.

FURTHER READING

Feigenbaum, E. A., and Feldman, J. (eds.), *Computers and Thought*, New York and London, McGraw-Hill, 1963

Foss, B. (ed.), *New Horizons in Psychology*, Penguin, 1966

George, F. H., *The Brain as a Computer*, Pergamon Press, 1961

Pask, G., 'Machines that Teach', *New Scientist*, 1961, 16, pp. 308–11

INDEX

MORE ABOUT PENGUINS
AND PELICANS

Penguinews, which appears every month, contains details of all the new books issued by Penguins as they are published. From time to time it is supplemented by our stocklist, which includes almost 5,000 titles.

A specimen copy of *Penguinews* will be sent to you free on request. Please write to Dept EP, Penguin Books Ltd, Harmondsworth, Middlesex, for your copy.

In the U.S.A.: For a complete list of books available from Penguins in the United States write to Dept CS, Penguin Books, 625 Madison Avenue, New York, New York 10022.

In Canada: For a complete list of books available from Penguins in Canada write to Penguin Books Canada Ltd, 2801 John Street, Markham, Ontario L3R 1B4.

ORDER AND DISPUTE

An Introduction to Legal Anthropology

Simon Roberts

Simon Roberts contends that legal theory has become too closely identified with arrangements in western societies to be of much help in cross-cultural studies of order. After all, there are many societies which survive in a remarkably orderly way without the help of judges, law-courts and policemen. But conversely, by looking at ways in which these other societies keep order and solve disputes, he shows that they can give us valuable guidance in the contemporary debate about order in our own society.

POWER POLITICS

Martin Wight

Power Politics provides a historical introduction to the cardinal principles of international politics. Concentrating not on the ephemera of current events but on the features of international politics that are fundamental and enduring, Martin Wight has written a classical account of the international system that arose in Europe at the start of the modern era, spread itself over other continents, and still provides the political framework of the world.

WHITE MAN, WE WANT TO TALK TO YOU

Denis Herbstein

The Soweto uprising marked the emergence of a generation of black students who have assimilated the new confidence inspired by the Black Consciousness philosophy. The enforced use of Afrikaans as a medium of school instruction was for them a challenge to be met initially by peaceful protest, but, in the face of vicious reaction from white authorities, in a fury of retribution. Denis Herbstein offers first-hand, factual reporting of the events in the townships, police stations, courts and in parliament. Together with the incorporated texts of conversations that he held with both black and white, he builds up a portrait of a troubled country which is neither pretty nor reassuring.

FACT AND FICTION IN PSYCHOLOGY

H. J. Eysenck

This is the final volume of Professor Eysenck's Pelican trilogy: *Uses and Abuses of Psychology, Sense and Nonsense in Psychology* – and now *Fact and Fiction in Psychology*.

The author's style is as incisive and his wit as keen as ever, while the range of subjects that he deals with is, as always, provocatively wide. Of special interest in this volume is his application of behavioural therapy to the theory and practice of neurotic behaviour and especially to the severe clinical problem of the alcoholic. Professor Eysenck's most recent views on the criminal personality are set out with challenging authority.

Further chapters on the psychology of road traffic offenders and a hard look at the more exclusive claims of depth psychology complete a fascinating volume.

Also published

USES AND ABUSES OF PSYCHOLOGY
SENSE AND NONSENSE IN PSYCHOLOGY
KNOW YOUR OWN I.Q.
CHECK YOUR OWN I.Q.